A SHORT ACCOUNT
OF WEST AFRICA'S GOLD COAST
AND ITS NATURE

A SHORT ACCOUNT OF WEST AFRICA'S GOLD COAST AND ITS NATURE

ERICK TILLEMAN

Translated from Danish and edited by
SELENA AXELROD WINSNES

DIASPORIC AFRICA PRESS

This book is a publication of
DIASPORIC AFRICA PRESS
NEW YORK | WWW.DAFRICAPRESS.COM
© Diasporic Africa Press, 2013

First published under the title, *En Kort Og Enfoldig Beretning Om Det Landskab Guinea Og Dets Beskaffenhed* (1697) – *A Short and Simple Account of The Country Guinea and its Nature*, translated and edited by Selena A. Winsnes, through the African Studies Program, University of Wisconsin-Madison, 1994.

Diasporic Africa Press Edition

All rights reserved. No part of this publication may be reproduced or distributed in any form or by any means, or stored in a database or retrieval system, without the prior written permission of the publisher.

ISBN-13 978-1-93730609-0 (pbk.: alk paper)
Library of Congress Control Number: 2013950999

CONTENTS

INTRODUCTION	i
CHAPTER ONE	
About the Country Guinea	1
CHAPTER TWO	
From the Rio Sierra Leone	
to the Greyn [Grain] Coast	7
CHAPTER THREE	
Greyn [Grain] Coast	11
CHAPTER FOUR	
Tusk and Quaqua Coasts	17
CHAPTER FIVE	
Gold Coast	21
CHAPTER SIX	
Acara [Accra]	33
CHAPTER SEVEN	
About the Kingdom Acara	37
CHAPTER EIGHT	
About the gold on the Gold Coast	
and other places in the land	43
CHAPTER NINE	
About the Slave Trade	47
CHAPTER TEN	
About religion, crops, animals, fish, reptiles	51
CHAPTER ELEVEN	
The wares carried from Europe to Guinea	
and traded there	61
CHAPTER TWELVE	
Conclusion	65

APPENDICES

Chronology of the Three Castles	71
Glossary	73
Bibliography	77
Index	85
Notes	97

INTRODUCTION

I
Background

Denmark-Norway was penultimate among the European nations to enter the frenetic fray that was the trade on the Gold Coast in the seventeenth century, and by the time of its arrival in 1658, six other nations were already actively engaged in trade.[1] Having started there in the 1470s, Portugal had long enjoyed a monopoly on the Gold Coast, and then lost it to the Dutch by their capture of the fort at Elmina in 1637, and the fort at Axim in 1642. However, operating from their well-established bases on Cape Verde on the Upper Coast, São Tome in the Bight of Biafra, and from Angola, Portuguese ships continued very much in evidence all along the coast. Spain's interest in sub-Saharan Africa had started in the 1450s, and its ships traded along the coast in competition with Portugal from 1475. But Spain had then given up all claims under the four treaties signed at Alcáçovas in 1479.[2] France started her activities in Guinea in *ca*. 1500. Operating along the Upper Coast (Senegambia to Sierra Leone) she was engaged both in peaceful trade as well as in the seizure of cargo from Portuguese ships. However, Portugal, by patrolling until the 1530s, was able to keep the French from the Mina coast, the chief trading place for gold.[3] The English had sent their first ship in 1530 but did not become actively involved in trading until 1553. They stayed on to become a contender against Portugal and the Netherlands, in the three-way rivalry for hegemony in trade on the Gold Coast.[4] The Dutch arrived in the 1590s but not until the creation of the Dutch West India Company in 1621 did they make their presence seriously felt.[5]

Thus the English and the Dutch became, and remained, the chief rivals for establishments and trade on the Gold Coast. Sweden sent its first ship in 1646, established a fort and lodges, and continued trading until 1658 when Henrik Carlof took over on behalf of the Danes. Although the forts and trading posts were

i

restored to Sweden in 1660, losses had been too great and the Swedish Africa Company closed down in 1663.[6] The Brandenburgers were the last arrivals. Their first trip was in 1681 and they built a fort and two lodges on the Gold Coast in 1683 and 1686, which they held until 1718 and 1721.[7]

The mid-seventeenth century saw the scramble for trading privileges well and truly launched. Gold, formerly the chief article of trade, now had to share pride of place with the trade in slaves. Taking their cue from the example of the Dutch West India Company, similar companies were created by the other European nations.[8] The Danish King Frederik III in (1648-70) gave the Glückstadt Company its charter in 1659. Not only did these countries benefit from the example of the company system, they also benefited from Dutch individual expertise and capital. In many cases Dutch traders, restive under the constraints of the company monopoly, began to operate on their own and offered their services to other countries. The same was the case with the merchants who invested in the ventures of other countries. It is not strange that individual traders, alumni, as it were, of the Dutch Company, very frequently turn up, both as interlopers, and as active participants in the operations of other countries. Each company felt an acute need for bases on land, such as lodges, factories, and forts for several reasons: as depots; for living quarters for representatives of the company; as bases for meetings with the African chiefs, merchants, and negotiators, since their ships had to be anchored in the roads and could not easily serve as meeting places; and, not least, to reify their presence, well-armed, as an effective means of keeping competitors away.

Rivalry between the companies of different nations, as well as between companies and interlopers, was reboant and methods were often underhanded. I shall recount the history of Cape Coast Castle below for two reasons; it is germane to the Tilleman text, and it is an excellent example of the methods employed in the struggle for a foothold on the Coast. The consent and support of the African leaders and their people were *sine quibus non*, and the latter were knowledgeable in profiting by this requirement. It was they who leased (some Europeans claimed "sold") the sites for construction of factories and forts. They determined the amount of tribute to be paid; they controlled the supplies of slaves and gold from the interior; they could use the European presence to advantage *vis-à-vis* their own enemies; they could—and did—play the Europeans against each other to their own advantage. And the Europeans often had to tread a very narrow path between African polities.⁹ The heightening of European rivalry made it impossible for the three leading contenders—Netherlands, England and France—to exercise complete control each for its own nation, thus making it possible for the smaller nations—Sweden, Denmark-Norway, and Brandenburg—to move in, all building bases on the Coast.

Most of the more than 60 establishments of various sizes that were built on the Gold Coast in the course of 300 years were in existence by the beginning of the eighteenth century. The reason for this concentration precisely on the Gold Coast was twofold: the rocky, promontory coast lent itself to the construction of permanent buildings, in contrast to the sandy lagoon coast to the west and the delta area to the east; and the Africans living there were, by then, experienced and knowledgeable in commerce with the Europeans. Desiring contact which would ensure and expand trade, they were willing, in return for compensation and tribute, to allow the Europeans to build forts and lodges.

II
History of Cape Coast Castle

Overseas trade from Denmark-Norway to Asia and Africa existed from early in the seventeenth century. Christian IV (1588-1648) had given a charter to the East India Company in 1616, and trade was centered around Tranquebar in India, but extended to the Spice Islands. Expeditions had also been sent to Greenland, and a trade monopoly with Iceland was in effect. The first ventures into the Guinea trade were small but showed tantalizing possibilities. Private Danish traders had taken slaves from Guinea to the West Indies in the 1650s.¹⁰ Sweden, Denmark's ancient and constant rival, had already built a factory, Carolusborg, near

Cape Coast in 1653, as well as three lodges. Denmark-Norway's establishment on the Gold Coast began before the founding of its first company. It began with the takeover of Carolusborg from the Swedes who had built it. The history of that fort and its transformation from being a Swedish lodge to becoming the main fort of the English in the space of twelve clamorous years is the tale of European rivalry and scheming both in Europe and Africa, African alliance and participation, conflicts between companies and private ventures—the tale of the way things were on the Gold Coast in the seventeenth century.

Swedish enterprise in Guinea started with expeditions financed by Louis de Geer, the "iron king" in Sweden and a director of the Dutch West India Company, in 1647. This, and several other successful expeditions the next two years resulted in the chartering of the (Swedish) African, Asiatic, and American Trading Company in 1649. On one of his voyages to Guinea, Captain Arent Gabbesen, sailing for de Geer, met Henrik Carlof, a Pole employed by the Dutch West India Company, and a man of many connections with Africans on the Coast. Carlof helped Gabbesen establish trade by negotiating with the king and chief minister of Fetu on his behalf. Carlof, undoubtedly enticed by an irresistible offer, left the Dutch company, returned to Europe with Gabbesen, and joined the Swedes. He was appointed director of the Swedish Company in 1649 and sailed to Fetu, renewing his contacts there. King Bodema/Bredva of Fetu gave him permission to build a lodge. The year of its founding is given variously as 1652, 1653, and 1655, and it was named Carolusborg in honor of Karl X Gustaf, king of Sweden from 1654 to 1660.[11] Carlof returned to Europe in 1655, leaving Carolusborg in the charge of Johan Philip von Krustenstjerna.

Meanwhile Louis de Geer, Carlof's friend and patron, had died and Carlof fell out with the heirs. Denmark-Norway was preparing for a war against their traditional enemy, Sweden-Finland, and the Dutch, favoring the Danes (perhaps thinking them weaker than Sweden and subsequently easier to control in Guinea) gave them financial aid. Carlof, disenchanted with the Swedish company, joined the Danes and set out for the Gold Coast, in December 1657, to capture Carolusborg for the Danish company.

It was claimed that at his first stop, a Swedish lodge west of Cape Three Points, he raised the Swedish flag thus enticing a Swedish representative aboard. He detained the man to get information on conditions at Carolusborg. The story may be apocryphal but it is thoroughly credible because Tilleman warns his readers several times not to trust the show of colors.

Having been provided with extra ships and manpower by the Dutch at Axim, and with support from Elmina, Carlof contacted Jan Claessen (Acrosan) the Dey (Chief Minister) of Fetu and brother of the king. Carlof reminded the Dey of an earlier agreement that Carlof be given the Swedish possessions when he claimed them. He also promised to cancel all Jan Claessen's debts to Sweden if he and the Fetu would assist Carlof in the takeover of Carolusborg. The promise was patently fraudulent because Carlof was now in the Danish service, a fact of which the Dey must have been unaware. The agreement was between him and Carlof personally, placing the fort in Carlof s hands alone.[12] Despite stiff resistance, Carolusborg was captured, Krustenstjerna was taken prisoner, and a Swedish ship, *Stockholm Slott*, lying at anchor in the road with a very rich cargo, was confiscated and the Danish flag hoisted to its mast. Carlof's deed; the subsequent demand from Sweden that Carlof be arrested as a pirate and the Swedish ship and cargo returned; Carlofs last-minute nocturnal escape with the ship—all were instrumental in the start of the new war between the two countries.[13] The war ended in 1660 and compensation to Sweden was agreed on.

Carlof had settled in Antwerp but was contacted by the newly-formed Danish Glückstadt Company because the fort was still in his hands by agreement with the Fetu. With Sweden still after him, he agreed to transfer ownership to Denmark in return for a promise of protection, that is, a confirmation that he had been acting on the orders of the Danish king; and that he could continue to enjoy trading privileges on the Coast. His demands were met and he did indeed continue trading privately by contract with both the French and Dutch for another twenty years. Thus was the career of one of the most illustrious of the Dutch Company's alumni.

But what of Carolusborg? Samuel Schmidt, yet another Hollander, had been left in charge of the Danish fort and lodges by Carlof in 1658. In 1659 Schmidt was purportedly convinced by the Dutch that Denmark had been conquered by Sweden and that the Danish Company no longer existed. As a consequence, according to this story, he handed over the Danish possessions to the Dutch. Schmidt himself, however, reported that he had been in dire circumstances: none of the supply ships that Carlof had promised had come; provisions and trade goods were lacking; the men at Carolusborg, harassed and threatened by the Fetu, were frightened and helpless; the Dutch Director-General Caspar van Houssen was offering gifts if Schmidt and his factors would give over the fort and join the Dutch Company. Carolusborg was now Dutch.[14]

The most influential man at Cape Coast (many said the entire Gold Coast) was Acrosan/Jan Claessen, the Dey of Fetu. He was displeased with this exchange, besieged the fort, and ousted the Dutch. Still favorably disposed toward the Swedes, he urged them to send a ship and take possession again. This was done in 1660, on payment to the Dey of 27,000 specie dollars in gold and the commitment to hire some 40 Africans at a high monthly salary. The Swedes held the fort under a commandant named Anthony Voss until after the death of Jan Claessen in 1662, but the Fetu were becoming increasingly dissatisfied at the continuing lack of Swedish supply ships, which were undoubtedly being hindered by a Dutch blockade. With Jan Claessen out of the picture the Fetu took charge again in 1663, evidently by a ruse. They entered the fort on the pretense of conducting friendly business, took over, and confiscated all the gold and goods, including those placed there by the Danes from their Fort Frederiksborg on the hill above Carolusborg.

Now the Danes, English, and Dutch were all competing for permission from the Fetu to have control of Carolusborg, and it was the Dutch who won the day—on condition that they remain at peace with their European neighbors. Having given the promise they proceeded to break it. They imprisoned and maltreated Anthony Voss, who eventually escaped and returned to Sweden.[15] Finally, after litigation in Europe, the Dutch paid compensation to Sweden, thus bringing to an end in 1663 Swedish involvement in the Guinea trade, and Carolusborg was again Dutch.

The final installment in the saga of Carolusborg needs a description of its neighbor, the Danish Fort Frederiksborg.[16] In 1659 the newly-chartered (Danish) Glückstadt Company, ignorant of the Dutch takeover six months earlier, sent Jost Cramer (a native of Frankfurt and yet another former employee of the Dutch West India Company) to be commandant at Carolusborg. Finding the Dutch ensconced there under the command of Caspar van Houssen, Cramer started negotiations with the Fetu for a new establishment. The king of Fetu, Hennique, gave the Danes permission to build on Mount Manfro, as well as rights to its coast and harbor, and a lodge near Cape Coast. Fort Frederiksborg was built on the hill approximately one kilometer east of Cape Coast, and named in honor of Frederik III, king of Denmark-Norway from 1648 to 1670. There was constant conflict between the Danes and the Dutch at Carolusborg, largely manifested by attacks, counterattacks, and confiscation of ships in the road. The Dutch maintained that in reality the Glückstadt Company was not Danish at all, but composed of Dutchmen whose purpose was to circumvent the restrictions of the Dutch company. Given the personnel, the complaint was not unreasonable.

Not only was the tension between the Danes and the Dutch unremitting, but rivalry between the English and the Dutch had been increasing during these years. The English Company of Royal Adventurers, incorporated in the 1660s and granted a long-term monopoly on trade, sought aid from their king because English ships, defying a Dutch blockade off the coast of Fetu, were either being seized or driven away. As a result, an English fleet commanded by Captain Robert Holmes was sent out against the Dutch possessions in 1664 and succeeded in taking all of them along the coast from Gorée and southward and eastward, apart from Elmina. Holmes' appearance was particularly timely for the Danes, whose Fort Frederiksborg was under attack by the Dutch at Carolusborg. The Danes then allied themselves with the English, and together with assistance from the Fetu, a coordinated attack was launched on Carolusborg—by the English from the sea, by the Danes from their hill, and by the Fetu from the surrounding land. The Dutch surrendered after eight days. Now the English Royal Adventurers were in control at Carolusborg and the Danes were safe at Frederiksborg. The Netherlands responded by sending a fleet under Admiral Michael Adrianzoon de Ruyter the following year. They recovered most of the lodges/forts previously lost to Holmes but made no attempt on Carolusborg, now reinforced and renamed Cape Coast Castle.

The final chapter of this tale was the loss of the Danish headquarters at Fort Frederiksborg twenty-three years later. The Glückstadt Company was failing and desperate in 1672. There were no wares for trade, no money at the fort; they felt threatened by their African neighbors; the new English Royal African Company, established that year and in possession of Cape Coast Castle, had embarked on a more aggressive trade rivalry. The fort was decaying physically, yet elegant and impressive entertainment of guests was evidently not curtailed.[17] The commander at Frederiksborg had been borrowing money from his English neighbors, and by 1679 the fort was deeply in debt. Hans Lykke, appointed commander in 1684, finally pawned the fort to the English Company factor, Henry Nurse. The English took possession in 1685, renaming it Fort Royal. They had desired ownership of the fort for several years for the defense of Cape Coast Castle from land. The final transfer was made in 1688 with a payment to the Danes of £900, and cancellation of their debt. The Danes then moved to their Fort Christiansborg at Osu, made it their new headquarters, and from then on concentrated their trade eastward toward the Volta River and beyond, to the Slave Coast.

Christiansborg Castle changed hands several times in the next decade, being at one time in the hands of Portugal and another time in the hands of the powerful Akwamu. Although the land for the building of Christiansborg had been made available by the king of Accra in 1661, by the time of Tilleman's arrival in 1697 it was with the inland state of Akwamu that the Europeans had to deal. Akwamu, a nation from the interior, had conquered Accra in 1680, thus becoming a coastal nation, and it remained the most powerful nation around the Accra area until its defeat by another inland nation, Akim, in 1730. For the history of Christiansborg Castle see Chapter 6.

III
Tilleman on the Coast

By 1689 the Glückstadt Company was heavily in debt and powerless to function. Nicolas Jansen Arf, one of the leading shipowners in Copenhagen, stepped into the breach. He applied for, and received for himself and his heirs, exclusive rights to trade in Guinea, including privileges to control all Danish possessions there. This arrangement shifted the trade from
Glückstadt to Copenhagen.[18] A final attempt to salvage the trade for Glückstadt was made by Thomas Thors, a veteran Guinea trader. After paying Arf for permission to trade in Guinea he sailed in 1690 on the *Charlotta Amalia*. This was the ill-fated voyage on which the ship was seized by English pirates, renamed the *Bachelors' Delight,* and achieved fame as a privateer.[19]

Under Arf's agent, Nickolai Fensman, Christiansborg Castle was completed by the construction of the fourth bastion, materials having been brought from Denmark. Nonetheless, a new commandant, Harding Petersen, installed in 1692, was evidently not strong enough to resist a takeover by the Akwamu in June 1693. The Akwamu traded freely from the Castle with English and Dutch ships until December 1693 when the merchants Hartwig Meyer and Johan Trane arrived from Europe in Arf's three ships. It was not until their arrival at Accra that they learned that the Akwamu were in possession of Christiansborg. They asked for, and received, aid from the Dutch at Fort Crèvecoeur at Accra. By negotiations the castle was returned to the Danes, but one of the ships, the *Christiansborg,* was captured by pirates on the way home. The financial losses sustained by Arf due to the Akwamu takeover and the loss of the ship were catastrophic, putting an end to his business.

Since Denmark was still interested in maintaining trading stations in Guinea and in supplying slaves for its planters on St.

Thomas in the West Indies, the trade was reopened in 1696 after three years of inactivity. The West India-Guinea Company was chartered in 1697, to be managed by the merchant Jens Juel and Privy Councilor Mathias Moth, who were given the right to enter into alliances with African states.[20] All other European and Danish subjects were barred from trading at Christiansborg. In 1697 the ship *Københavns Børs* was sent out to take over for the company. Erick Tilleman was aboard as their special agent. He had served in the Guinea trade earlier, and now he was given the difficult task of bringing about order at Christiansborg. Under his direction the garrison was strengthened, new agreements were made with the Akwamu king, new supplies were provided, and Arf's temporary commandant, Erick Lygaard, was appointed governor by Tilleman on behalf of the Company. The fort was officially handed over to the West India-Guinea Company (Copenhagen) in December 1698. It was now stronger and better equipped than its neighbors, the English James Fort and the Dutch Fort Crèvecoeur. Tilleman's mission had been accomplished.

IV
The Book and the Text

Little is known of Tilleman beyond the following facts: he was an army officer, commissioned lieutenant in 1687 in Drabantgarden, second lieutenant in an infantry regiment in 1687. One source states that he had been *kommandant* at Christiansborg for nine years; another simply that he made three voyages to West Africa between 1682 and 1689, and lived there for a total of nine years. I have been unable to find any more information.[21]

En kort og enfoldig Beretning om det Landskab Guinea og dets Beskaffenhed, "A short and simple account of the country Guinea and its nature." This book, published in 1697, is precisely what the author intended it to be. It is short—163 octavo pages. It is simple. It is "not presented in an elevated historical style and with great eloquence...." It is intended to give useful information to captains and merchants sailing to Guinea to trade—a pilot. It is in effect a forerunner to the modern "post description" sent from international organizations to their representatives going into the field. But is it significant for the twentieth-century student of African history?

Its very existence is significant as yet another section of the historical frieze. The material is that of the end of the seventeenth century, the period when the dramatic changes that took place in the eighteenth century were beginning to materialize. The slave trade was to become the chief interest, the use of firearms was to become much more widespread. Tilleman's time on the Gold Coast came just after Barbot's and coincided with that of Phillips and Bosman. It is of interest to compare and contrast their reports to give us a fuller picture of events, practices, and allegations. A comparison of the areas in which they agree and where there are discrepancies would itself be worth a study, especially considering that these four men represent different European backgrounds, colored by their particular national interests. Why are some of the coastal people "good" for some writers and "bad" for others? How much is personal observation and how much is hearsay? How much is purposeful propaganda designed to keep potential competitors away? It is also important to note that the Europeans' headquarters on the Coast were in different places and among different nations: Barbot and Phillips used Cape Coast, among the Fetu, as their home base; Bosman lived and worked at Elmina among the Fante; Tilleman worked at Christiansborg among the Gã and Akwamu. Tilleman's book also reveals, as do the other sources, prevailing attitudes and beliefs held by the Europeans, as they described the Africans and their lives. Since Tilleman's purpose was to produce a practical guide to sailing and trade, his efforts in the areas of cultural and natural phenomena were clearly minimal. It follows that it was much easier to reiterate the general attitudes toward, for example, religious practices, the character of the people at various places, or supposed beliefs held by the Africans. His report on flora and fauna appears to be a nod in the direction of accepted practice—something one is expected to write about from mysterious Africa. But serious investigation was not part of Tilleman's authorship. He was a merchant, he was a sailor, and he genuinely wanted to share his knowledge in those fields.

It has been remarked that Tilleman plagiarized Müller extensively.[22] I have tried to discover which of the earlier writers Tilleman might have read, and "plagiarized" and it is certain that he was well-acquainted with Müller's book. One other certain acquaintance was with the sea charts and texts of the *Burning Fen,* an acquaintance he shared with the others sailing along the Guinea Coast.[23] The proof of his knowledge of, and access to, Müller's writing appears indisputably in his descriptions of fish on the Coast. But was it plagiarizing? He assiduously copied Müller's list, with only a few orthographical differences, but the descriptions were entirely his own. I suggest that he simply used the same listing, thus saving himself the trouble of noting and remembering which fish he had seen. Tilleman was, above all, a practical man and was undoubtedly happy not to have to expend unnecessary energy in the writing of material which was not of vital interest to him. In fact, one wonders why he did not go on to copy Müller's descriptions as well. The answer to that is his "short and simple" approach. Müller's descriptions were clearly too long and detailed. They both wrote about animals, birds, and plants too. In these areas, where Müller's listed and described in some detail, Tilleman went his own way. Animals and birds are cataloged in paragraph form and are often impossible to identify. His listing of food plants is different from Müller's, and his descriptions, like those of the animals and birds, are barely adequate for identification. In the few places where phrases are the same, they are descriptions or comparisons so common as to be insignificant as evidence of studied plagiarism.

It is said that Tilleman also "plagiarized" Müller in the telling of the history of Cape Coast Castle. Müller wrote an exciting and detailed account of the changes of ownership from 1653 to 1664. Tilleman wrote a précis. Although this history would have been common knowledge on the Gold Coast and in Europe, Tilleman, again, seems to have used Müller as a guide, picking out facts and the sequence of events, the bare bones. Practically the only place where the same, or nearly the same, words are used is in the telling of Captain Holmes' arrival at Cape Coast. Müller wrote, "...the Lord God granted us Danish servants at Friederichsburg a strange piece of help; for on 14 April of the said year an English fleet of thirteen strong warships and merchant ships under Admiral Robert Holms arrived...." Tilleman wrote, "...until GOD unexpectedly sent help, in that on 14 April the same year the English Admiral Robert Holms arrived to anchor in the road there with thirteen capital ships...."

I maintain that, given the gravity of the term today, an accusation of plagiarism is far too harsh. Tilleman had access to, and was using, an excellent source. Had he taken material from others to enhance his own work, to compensate for his own lack of talent as a writer, yes, it could be called plagiarism. But his intention was practically the opposite. He was not attempting to enthrall a general readership; rather, he was providing information for "specialists" who would themselves be visiting the area and could augment details as they wished. Thus he wanted to present the necessary facts as succinctly and simply as possible, and gladly left the creativity to others. But he neglected to name his source. Considering that copyright laws were not yet in existence, his was not a crime. It was at worst a mild misdemeanor, at best a fault.

V
The Translation

My translation has been kept as close to the original as possible in order that the flavor and the meaning of the text be preserved. Thus there has been no attempt to alter style or to edit for fluency. Original pagination is included in boldface square brackets, and paragraphing mimics the original. Sentence structure and phraseology have been maintained, but capitalization of nouns has been dropped. Where sentences are awkward or even enigmatic, I have attempted a translation based on informed guesses and have quoted the original in the notes. All personal names and toponyms in the original were printed in Roman script, in contrast to the text, which was in Gothic. I have emulated this visual contrast by using italics for names and terms in Roman script. Toponyms, if similar to modern forms, are identified at first appearance in [--], as far as identification is possible. If they are long, or need explanation, they are included in the notes. Certain terms, such as *Negeri* (Negro settlement) and *Natureller* (Natives) have been retained to preserve the flavor of the text. Where Tilleman refers to the Africans in other terms, I have followed his lead: *Negre* (Negroes), *Sorte* (Blacks), *Indvaanere* (inhabitants). By the same token, I have used the varying terms he used for the establishments: "fort," "fortress," and "castle." All material in parentheses are printed thus in the original text, while editorial comment is in square brackets. Double quotation marks are used for direct quotations only, whereas single quotation marks are used for vernacular usage when not in Roman script in the original.

The listing of sources in the notes requires comment. The modern sources are listed in order of publication date. The early sources, however, have been listed according to the original date of publication or the actual period covered, although modern dates for new editions are given. Thus all the sources in the Jones translations whose original publication dates are early seventeenth century, are listed on that basis with the modern publication date (1983). The Brandenburg sources, covering the late seventeenth century are identified with (1985). The same applies to De Marees, originally 1602, now (1987); Barbot, first published in 1732, now (1992); Isert, originally 1788, now (1992). The modern editions are not only more readily accessible, of course, but, being critical editions, have important commentary and supplementary material which will be of use to the modern reader.

CHAPTER ONE
About the Country Guinea

There are a number of opinions concerning the country *Guinea*, which lies on the southern side of *Africa*, and from which place on the coast it takes its beginning. Some insist that it begins at *Cabo Verde* [Cape Verde], which lies at fourteen and one-half degrees on the north *æquinoctial* line, which, however, seems to be somewhat too far [north][24] Others, on the contrary, say that it does not have its beginning before *Cabo* [2] *de Monte* [Cape Mount], which lies at 6 deg. 30 min., which is considered to be much too short [i.e. too far south]. But the Portuguese, who carry on their trade on its coast daily, and were the very first to sail that coast, starting in the year 1481, thus for more than two hundred years, reckon its beginning to be between the two aforementioned places; that is, at *Rio Sierra Liona* [Sierra Leone], which lies at 8 deg. 20 min., which I, myself, by my own experience, along with the majority and the most knowledgeable, consider to be the most correct.[25] For this reason no newly – arrived ship (the French and Portuguese excepted) would willingly put in to the coast or the country off more than [i. e. north of] 10 deg., unless it is a case of emergency or on specific orders.

Therefore, at present, the aforementioned French and Portuguese carry on trade at *Cabo Verde* and places in the vicinity virtually alone, and also, all along the rivers they have their lodges, [3] field redoubts, and fortresses, by means of which they do not permit any other nation to come [to these places].[26] It is chiefly the French who consider those [other nations] fair game whom they can take by surprise and overcome, either by stealth or by force, in that large *River Gambia*, which lies 30 miles [225 km.] from *Cabo Verde*. Which, indeed, a Brandenburg licensed sailor by the name of *Claus Bording* experienced in the year 1684, as several others have often done.[27]

From this *Cabo Verde* to *Cabo Tagrin* [Tagrin Point] it is a hundred miles and yet there are many places between them that are settled by the country's inhabitants, *Negroes* and *Blacks*, also called *Natureller* [Natives]. However, it is not on the coast that they live, but farther inland. And the Portuguese report in their descriptions that at all these places farther along, which lie between the aforementioned *Cabo Verde* and [4] *Cabo Tagrin,* and mostly where there are rivers, those same *Naturellerne* and country people live; that is, at *Cabo Verde,* where most of them are fishermen, at *Port Dale, Punte Legard, Souvalle, Borsalo, Rio Gambia,* which is populated everywhere, *Rio Cumba, St. Pedro, St. Anna, Ostras, Ile, Formosa, Buguba, Rio de Nuno, Rio des Ostras, Piedras, Cammekovv, Rio de Pogona, Fatima, Cagranco, Caces, Caracone,* and inland on *Cabo Tagrin* at *Porta.* But they are farther inland, as reported before, and hardly any at the coast.[28]

Among these [people] things are found to vary considerably in all ways at about every fourth mile, and they are quite without faith of any kind. They publicly worship the

Devil, whom they call *Commaté,* and make sacrifices to him.[29]

The wares which are found there, and particularly at *Rio Gambia,* are elephant teeth, elephant hides, [5] buffalo skins, *ambergris, civet,* wax, rice, redwood, cotton cloth, and mats, as well as some slaves, and a quantity of the country's fruits; which things one trades for *perpetuaner,* or *rask,* coarse canvas, iron, worked pewter of *manggods,* brass pans and cauldrons, bracelets of metal, and Portuguese tobacco.[30]

Nine miles from *Cabo Tagrin* is the river *Sierra Liona,* which is regularly visited by all newly arrived ships in need of water and fresh supplies, which one gets here, as well as at some other places along the entire *Coast.* And indeed such water here than which none can be found to be better in any river in all of Africa; for which reason the aforementioned places are not visited by the Danish, English, Dutch, or Brandenburg Guinea travelers.[31] Moreover, the real trade of the *Coast* is considered to begin at [6] *Cabo Messuratte* [Cape Mesurado], which is more than fifty miles from *Rio Sierra Liona,* so no one, if not in a case of extreme need, seeks land except where trade begins immediately.

That river [*Sierra Leone*] lies at 8 deg. 20 min. north latitude, west by northwest, and east by southeast, and there are very strong ebb and flood tides there. The following information should serve to aid ships putting in there: that one should normally always have flat water from *Katsøen* [Cacheo] right to that river itself. At the entrance it is 25, 22, 20, 18, 16, 15, 14, 12, and 10 fathoms deep and there is good bottom everywhere. When putting in at 9 deg. 12 min. one stands in close to the four islands and then south, well past the shallows of both rivers, which lie north of *Rio Sierra Liona*. Immediately thereafter one sees the high land of *Sierra Liona*, and [one] stands in right to [7] the southernmost edge, at which there lie two cliffs against which breakers can be seen. When one is past them one runs close along the shore, and there is very calm water due to a bank which extends from the northern edge, after which care must be taken, since ships have previously been damaged on this bank. And when one has run in a little farther one sees the large inlet with high water like a standing river [?]. One stands past this, too, coming immediately to a bay with red sandy bottom at the shore for a couple of ship's lengths, and just there is a watering place where one can anchor at 13 and 12 fathoms in good bottom. And there one can lie, safe from all winds, storm, and bad weather.[32]

It is delightful to see how a number of prominent marine officers, who have taken on water there, have carved their names in the hard stone; [8] among whom one finds the very famous *Mr. Admiral Ruyters, Robbert* [sic] *Holms* and the renowned pirate *Claus Compans*, who is said to have had certain of his haunts here, in his time, and retired here, along with the names of many others. And immediately close by there also stands a very large tree, [measuring] more than sixteen fathoms in the round (which probably seems unbelievable); on this, also, a number of names are found carved as mementos.[33]

The inhabitants, or *Naturellerne*, live a *cannon*-shot farther inland from that same watering-place, scattered several miles from one another. But the highest standing and most prominent among them, who are called *Cabusees* [headmen] and who are, so to speak, the others' superiors,[34] live three good *fierding-vei* southwest of that same watering-place; and at their town, but a little farther to the south, one gets very good oysters. These *Cabusees*, at the end of the year 1690, [9] were two Blacks by the names of *Emanuel* and *Thomisse*; and these two usually came aboard to receive a little gift, which they called their *custom*, be-

3

cause we were permitted to avail ourselves of water, firewood, and other things freely and unobstructed at the river.[35]

The wares available here are *civet*, elephant tusks, rice, mats made of reeds, and palmwine, for which one gives them iron, basins, and other such things. Available from them, in addition, are small *Steen-bukke* or deer, chickens, pawpaws, citrons, and other fruits of the land as fresh provisions, which are traded for knives, old linen, *fyrstaal*, and more of such things.[36]

Northeast of the anchoring place and the watering-place, a good one and one-half miles inland, the English live along the river, where they have their *lodge*, or field station, at which [10] are found ten small cannons, and, otherwise, it is staffed by 12 common soldiers, a merchant and four or five officers.[37] They always have a small ship of twenty or thirty lasts, by means of which they anchor and trade at those places between *Rio Sierra Liona* and *Cabo de Monte*, that is, in *Rio Gamboas, Serbera, Madrebomba, Paniha, Galinhos*, and other places in the vicinity.[38] And besides these, they have, here and there on the rivers, small field redoubts staffed by their people.

These same Christians do not fail to come aboard as soon as they have the feeling that we are friends, and from them, in return for victuals, brandy, and cloth, we receive a quantity of ivory, especially when there has not been a ship in the river for a long time. Occasionally they have a little gold with them, but it is not of any particular value. [11] Here one can by no means trust any foreign flag, since for the most part, because of the excellent water and good approach there are always ships in the river, both good and evil. Indeed there are certain examples that, because there was lacking a watchful eye here, one or another has come to grief, in fact has lost both ship and goods, which happened in the year 1693 to the experienced and eldest of the Guinea travelers from the north, *Thomas Thorsøn* from Glückstad [sic], with a Danish *commission*, in that his frigate, *Charlotta Amalia*, well-manned by thirty-six crew and passengers was neatly seized by a small English pirateer with a crew of four in the space of a moment, purely because he did not keep a watchful eye on them. With this frigate these same English pirates later did a great deal of damage along the entire *Coast*. Eventually they grew [12] to a party of four [ships] which cause a great interruption in trade, until the English *Commendeur Killegrevv* came to *Guinea* under orders and constantly pursued them from there to the island St. Thomas in the West Indies, where most of them caught fire, and finally all of them together were destroyed.[39]

Here the earth is much cultivated with rice, called *pegla*, by which *Naturellerne* sustain themselves.[40] Their weapons consist of hand assegais, or hand bows and arrows, and daggers of iron without any steel. And there are extremely few among them who know how to handle gunpowder and charge. Their condition, for both the one and the other, is one purely of need and poverty, and they always live completely satisfied in such a condition, without sorrow or worry, not thinking any further either of their beginning or their end. They clearly give Satan the honor [13] of being their creator and immortal God, and sacrifice to him without shame, saying that all the earth's products and fruits have come from him; but that thunder, lightning, rain, and storm come from the Whites or white people's God, with whom they want nothing to do. Moreover, they honor and worship the moon, as well, when it is new and full, as well as several stars. There are found a number among them who speak quite good Portuguese and are very trustworthy and decent in their trading and behavior, more so than the others living west of the river, which is the main reason that there are always found Christians here among them.[41]

The country is everywhere overgrown with forest and thickets of small undergrowth and bush, entangled with each other like some large heap of hops, in which are found great numbers of elephants, buffaloes, wild boars, [14] small deer, monkeys, crocodiles, and many evil snakes which cannot be destroyed because one cannot get to them. Yet the inhabitants constantly do their best to kill them on the occasions when they come into the cultivated land and their grain.

In the river there are found very good fish, such as *harders, saphor, corcobados,* and other varieties which are unknown here [in Denmark] and of which one can catch enough as long as one is provided simply with a boat for seining, in which the English

5

always occupy themselves in obtaining their food, to their greatest advantage.[42]

CHAPTER TWO

From the Rio Sierra Leone to the Greyn [Grain] Coast

After [**15**] one has left the river *Sierra Liona,* one stands past *Baixos* [*sic*] and *St. Anna* [Shoals of St. Ann], with the mainland on the port side as far as *Cabo de Monte,* and though there live *Naturelle*r at these places yet it is always inland and not at the coast; therefore one makes no attempt to trade here at all, apart from what the Portuguese and English with their small ships can do, which has been described before.[43]

This *Cabo de Monte,* which lies twenty-four miles from *Rio Sierra Liona,* at 6 deg. 30 min., is a high mountain and when one approaches from the west it looks like a helmet, but when one is nearly there [**16**] it becomes long, with a valley in the middle, and around it to the east and west there is flat land everywhere, overgrown with scrub and bush.

West of that *Cabo,* which stretches out to sea south and south to east, one anchors at 7 or 6 fathoms in clean sand bottom. But in the *travat* [season] or rainy season (which prevails in the month of May and lasts nearly until the beginning of October) one anchors at 12 to 10 fathoms because of the strong wind which blows a great deal on that *Coast.*[44]

The *Natureller* there are not much accustomed to the sea, therefore one must trade with them on land. For this reason, [**17**] as soon as they see any ship in the sea they immediately make signals by fire and smoke on land, in order to bring it in to them.[45] And there are only very few of them who can speak Portuguese. Their town lies northeast of the seashore, one and one-half miles inland, and their wares are rice and ivory as well as many fruits.[46] One can also get water here in case of necessity, but with great trouble.

The Portuguese write that these people have a king whom they call *Rahala,* who when he so desires can muster more than seven hundred men to wage war, all equipped with bows and arrows, but not with any shooting weapons.[47]

[18] In the year 1680, in the month of November, a Frenchman took away, by stealth, eighteen persons from these same *Natureller*, among whom were two of the king's family for which we Danes soon had to pay the penalty when we arrived on the 7 January 1681, with the ship *Havmanden*.[48] Yet we remained unharmed after we had given small gifts to the king and highest officials; and that they are still there is not beyond belief.[49]

From this *Cabo de Monte* the *Coast* stretches southeast by east for about ten miles of completely low land, overgrown everywhere with scrub and bush, right up to the river *St. Paulo* [St. Paul River], which is only [19] a small river. Just before this one can stand in as close to land as one wishes, that is, at 12, 10, 8, and 6 fathoms of water with excellent clean bottom everywhere.[50]

In the same river there is available a great deal of redwood, for which the English traded formerly and they had their people living there among the [local] inhabitants in order to buy ivory, rice, and that same redwood, for which almost no one else took the trouble to land there; and even in these times the situation is nearly the same.[51]

From this same river the land runs in a small curve to *Cabo Misserado* [Cape Mesurado], to which the course sets southeast for one and one-half miles, with low land as before. [20] That same *Cabo* is a high mountain of which the northern extremity is the highest and the southern side slopes at a slant down to the beach. Southward, from the sea, it looks reddish and appears to be an island since the low land cannot be seen on any of its sides.[52]

The inhabitants at that place are not to be trusted at all, since they have often behaved roguishly toward the Christians, especially when they guessed that one was going to leave and not trade any more; for which reason one should convince them that one is going to stay longer among them, and then go away during the night before they notice and realize it.[53]

[21] Their wares are mostly rice, and it is the best available on the entire *Coast*. Sometimes they have elephant tusks, but not often, because ships go there steadily. If none has been there for a long time one can usually get a great deal of rice, which happened to a Danish *commission*-sailor, Daniel Henricksøn, in

the year 1685, in the month of January, when, on the third day he acquired more than sixteen barrels of rice, each pound not costing as much as one and one-half shillings.[54]

One stays there, west of that *Cabo*, in an open roadstead but with good anchoring ground, and [one can] row in the shallop, without danger, right into land, where one finds the inhabitants with their wares gathered in [22] great quantities. Yet one should usually have some hand guns hidden in the shallop or boat, in the event something should start. And one should take care that they do not come between one's boat and the people who have gone ashore, since the best of them is a scoundrel who thinks of nothing but stealing.[55]

Immediately east of this place one begins to see taller forests than [those] west of it, right to the *Rio Svinko* [River Junk], which is eight miles from the above-mentioned *Cabo Misserado*. On the eastern and southern side of the same river stand a number of tall trees by which it can easily be recognized, and inland lie three high mountains, of which the one in the middle has [23] a valley. There one anchors at 10 fathoms, with the aforementioned tall trees to the northeast, and where one has good anchoring ground.[56]

CHAPTER THREE
Greyn [Grain] Coast[57]

It is reckoned that the beginning of the *Greyn Coast* is at this river *Iunk*, or *Svinko*, with *Rio del Punto* [sic], and there the inhabitants are like the ones described earlier, and one must trade with them in the same manner as with the former ones.[58]

When one has gone past *Rio Svinko*, in an easterly direction, one sees three more mountains, with a valley [i. e., saddle] between each of them, and from that river the course continues southeast by east to *Rio St. Jean*, which is eight miles from there; and on the way [24] one runs right past *Rio Corse, Petit Diepen, Tabo de Gravv* and *St. Pedro*, since there is no significant trade there.[59]

At this *Rio St. Jean* [River St. John] there stand some tall trees on a low bank, which shoot straight up out of the sea and can be seen at a great distance from land; and one can anchor very well just in front of them, at 10 to 9 fathoms in good ground.[60]

The inhabitants at this place are somewhat more trustworthy than the earlier ones, and are somewhat accustomed to the sea, so that they have canoes or small fishing canoes in which they sometimes come out to the ships. In the river there is a great deal of redwood and, at times there is available from the inhabitants some [25] *malleget* or *greye* [sic] (which is paradise-corn) as well as ivory; yet not often, since the Portuguese from *St. Thomé* and other places are always here, flitting about in their small boats and buying it all.

Immediately east of *Rio S. Jean* one can see a mountain which is curved much like a rainbow, since it is high in the middle and curves down at both ends. At its eastern end there is a cape which runs out into the sea, where there is a large town called *Tabokanen*.[61] As soon as one is past that town one sees *daabelt Land* all the way to *Rio de Sester* [River Sess], which is reckoned to be a distance from *Rio St. Jean* southeast by east of 10 miles, and 6 miles from *Tabokanen*;[62] yet, [26] between *Tabokanen* and *Rio de Sester* there is another town called *Petit Dilps* [?], and there are rocks in the sea at both these towns, which are the first on the *Greyn Coast*.⁶³

When one comes to *Rio de Sester* there is a large plain and flat land which runs a good one and one-half miles out to sea, and the water's depth there is not more than 7 and seven and one-half fathoms deep, which makes this place easy to recognize. And running from there, east of the river, there is a rocky reef which is also a good landmark for this place.⁶⁴ One must be very careful at both these grounds when standing from the west, and when one wants to anchor at the river one runs over the first ground toward [27] the other, which is the aforementioned reef, at 7 and 8 fathoms. One then comes immediately to 14 and 15 fathoms with good bottom, and the closer to the reef the better, yet not too close since there are some hidden rocks; indeed, just there and close in to land one can see the surf breaking on them.⁶⁵

Three miles upriver lies a large town called *Kongens Plats*, where there are usually both good trade and good people to deal with, so that a ship newly arrived there is normally not in want of water, supplies, wood, and other things, for which reason one does not willingly run past this good trading place without orders. And there are [28] some rocks in the river, near which one rows in on the eastern side for the sake of going the shortest way.⁶⁶

Barely one and one-half miles from that river there is a rock on which there is a single tree, and hard by it lies a town called little *Sester*, at which, however, there is no business to be done.

Somewhat farther east, past *Cabo de Baikos Svino* and the so-called *White Rock* there lies another rock which resembles a sailing ship.⁶⁷ And even a little farther away there is a large rock from which a reef goes a good mile out to sea. As soon as one is past that one sails right towards land, where one [29] immediately sees a bush and some tall trees standing at the sea side, of which there are particularly three or four which are much taller than all the others, and near this there lies a town called *Sangvin* [Sangwin], which was, earlier, the best trading place on the entire *Greyn Coast*, but is not so much so now. This is reckoned to lie somewhat more than five miles' distance from *Rio de Sester,* and one anchors there at 16 fathoms in rocky ground. [68]

Even more easterly there is a trading place *Bottava* [Bottowa] on the way to which one runs past *Baffa Setterna* and *Dasso,* since these are only two small towns where the inhabitants themselves have canoes or small boats in which they [30] always come far out to sea if they have something to trade. And at that same *Bottava* there is a mountain close to the shore, across from which there is a rock, and along the shore there is very high land, all of which together are recognizable landmarks of that town; and one anchors near the mountain at ten fathoms in good ground. [69]

Still a little farther there lies another town by the name of *Sina* where, at present, there is also usually good trade.

From *Bottava* the coast stretches east-southeast for about five miles past *Sabrabon* [Blabar], to *Setter* and *Cru* [Settra Kru], at which there are scarcely any landmarks because the land itself has much [31] the same appearance everywhere, moreover it is very low compared to the other land [before this]. Yet, both at *Setter* and *Cru* there stand a group of tall trees pointed like ships' masts, or [looking] like ships whose masts alone are visible, and west of these there are a number of rocks which, along with the trees, one can see from a distance of many miles.[70] And, if one wants to anchor one must not come closer to land than ten fathoms' depth because there is foul ground at these places, where there is always good trade.[71]

From *Cru* and past *Badu* the *Coast* stretches southeast-east and east-southeast for about five miles to *Wappa* ['Wappo], [32] a good trading place for *greyn.* At that town there is the largest rock on the entire *Greyn Coast,* and yet it does not protrude much over the water; and around it there are a great number of both visible and hidden rocks. When one wants to anchor there one must sail past the large rock, keeping it to the north-northeast, where one can anchor at twenty fathoms in good ground, even though ground of small stones is found in some places.[72]

If one wants to get drinking water there one must keep all the rocks to the port side and row right up to a large tree with a round crown. As soon as one reaches land [33] one sees a round rock which is quite white from bird droppings, which one also keeps on the port side. But on the starboard side there is another rock whose eastern end is connected to land, along whose western edge one rows up to the aforementioned white one, where one finds a small bay where the boat can lie safely and free, and right at that spot the water comes flowing out of the bushes. But, since it is a little brackish one usually carries the barrels up into the town and lets the Blacks fill them, for which one gives them a few glass beads. And in much the same way good, fresh water can be obtained at *Setter* and [34] *Cru* when one has need of it.

It is a distance of six miles from *Wappa* to *Grand Setter* [Grand Sesters], which is a very good trading place where there are very good people to deal with, and the course sets east-southeast and southeast by east. One and one-half miles west of this town one sees a number of rocks as well as the one just outside of it, and hard by it there is also a tree which is divided into two parts and looks much like a windmill; which two things are those which one will notice first. In addition, close to that [divided tree], there are two or three trees, of which the westernmost is [35] quite without leaves. A mile farther away, in the east, there is a mountain close to the shore, and opposite that a small red cliff on which the aforementioned town of *Grand Setter* lies, so that that same red cliff is also a good landmark for it.[73]

If anyone wants to anchor there he must see to it that the aforementioned cleft tree is directly north of him, then he can anchor at sixteen and seventeen fathoms. And if anyone there should wish to get fresh water or to go ashore, the Blacks will come in great numbers of canoes and small boats to show him the way.

From *Grand Setter* to *Riaven, Griaven,* or *Goyan* [36] the course runs as before, southeast by east and east-southeast. At this place there is a round mountain about a cannon shot inland from the shore, and when this is visible in the east-northeast one anchors at thirteen or fourteen fathoms with good sand bottom; and then, to the south, one can also see the breakers on the reef of *Cabo Palma*.[74]

Here it is good to get water and wood, since there is a small river up which one can row in a boat or sloop! One keeps all the cliffs to starboard, or south, rows due west towards land, and anchors in the deepest water one can find, since at the seashore the ground is flat and sandy. [37] When one enters, the river is somewhat foul because of rocks and sand banks. Yet one can come right through quite well, until one finds some houses, where there is good water and wood, and good folk living there.[75]

From there to *Cabo de Palma* which lies at 4 deg. 15 min., one sails south-southeast and southeast by east, in order to stand well past the abovementioned reef, which stretches from that Cabo a mile out to sea. One must not come closer than fifteen to sixteen fathoms, since the rocks are aslant. At the outermost point of that same *Cabo* there is a round bush which, at first sight, looks like a [38] hill, until one comes closer to it; and behind this there is an elongated mountain which is not very high, yet higher than the aforementioned bush. One does not come here often because of the foul anchoring ground, as well as because the trade here is but very poor.[76]

This *Cabo de Palma* marks the end of the *Greyn Coast* or *Malleget Coast* trade which one enjoys most at *Setter, Cru, Wappa, Grand Setter*, and *Goyan*. The best times of the year to arrive there are from December to the month of May, when one usually has good weather everywhere on that coast.[77] Along the aforementioned places an easterly and westerly moon causes high tides. The people in that land are all [39] well accustomed to the sea so they come a good two or three miles out to sea in their canoes or boats; and if one does not want to anchor one can let the ship simply float slowly past the land where the aforementioned places are, and in good weather the Blacks usually come right on board.[78]

One must examine the *malleget* well on purchase to make sure that [what is] down at the bottom of the basket is not old or rotten. Even though these *Natureller* or inhabitants have experienced much pain because of such treachery, still, at times, they do not refrain; apart from that, one knows of no Christian nation that has experienced any wrong at the hands of these [40] inhabitants, from *Rio S. Jean* to this *Cabo de Palma*.

⊰ CHAPTER FOUR ⊱
Tusk and *Quaqua* Coasts[79]

The *Tusk Coast* is reckoned to have its beginning east of *Cabo de Palma* [Cape Palmas], and its inhabitants are evil, wicked people who aspire to harm all those whom they see. Indeed, according to certain reports, they have often overtaken small ships in their harbors and rivers and murdered many of the people on them.[80]

Two miles east of the aforementioned *Cabo* lies a town by the name of *Galrivoy*, or *Grova*, where there is usually good trade.[81] And that same *Cabo* stretches eastward about four miles and then northeast by east – northeast for close to twenty miles, to [41] *Tabo*, or *Tabotré* [Tabu]. But before one arrives there, there is still another town, called *Tabodue*, which, however, has no trade.[82]

West of *the aforementioned Tabotré* there is a point which slopes at a slight slant down into the sea, and on its outermost tip there stands a tree which is a good landmark for that trading place; and three miles east of the point there is a large round rock which is the first one lying east of *Cabo de Palma*; and even farther east of that rock there is a mountain sloping down to the sea.[83] But there is no sand ground at the beach here, but it is completely rocky. One can anchor at *Tabotré* [42] at twelve or fourteen fathoms in clay ground, after having run past the abovementioned tree on the point, keeping it to the northwest.

There are also, between *Cabo de Palma* and *Rio St. Andreas* [River Sassandra], a number of small places, such as *Taho*, *Pitero*, *Sitro*, and *Berby*, but these are all towns of no significant trade, therefore one usually does not anchor at those places, since the inhabitants always own canoes, by means of which they themselves manage to come aboard in sufficient numbers when they have tusks or other things to trade.[84]

From *Berby* the coast stretches east and east by south four miles to a lovely trading place which lies a couple of miles [43] west of *Rio St. Andreas*, *Dorvvyn* or *Druyden* [Drewin] by name, near which, east of it, there stands a tall, bare, leafless tree [*sic*]; and close to town, on a flat mountain, yet another large tree, with leaves. In addition, in a small valley there are two palm trees, which one shall sail past until they are lined up, giving the appearance of one tree, then keeping the other tree, on the mountain, to the north-northwest, one can anchor at thirteen and fourteen fathoms in good ground.[85]

When one is lying at anchor at this *Dorvvyn* one can see, at a distance of one and one-half miles to the east, the western bank of *Rio St.* [44] *Andreas*, which is high and sloping, behind which, before the *travat* or rainy season, there is good water and wood to be had, as long as one is on guard against the inhabitants' roguery and tyranny.[86]

At *Rio St. Andreas* the bottom is somewhat flat, so that when one is anchored at 12 fathoms one is still a good two miles from land, yet it is all clean, sandy bottom so that one can run in as close to land as one wishes; and in that river the water is eleven feet deep, but a little farther upriver it is quite dry. It divides into two parts; one runs west-northwest and the other northeast; and at times there is good trade in elephant tusks here.[87] [45] Right close to that place there is an inlet, so that the southern part of the land extends directly south-southeast out to the northern part of the land, and it is called *Roo Cleven*, or "red cliffs", since there are some red rocks in front of it;[88] and there is also a stand of four or five trees in a valley, where there is a town called *Sabatra*, and a little distance from there is another town by the name of *Domera*, where one acquires tusks, at times. And the course there from *Rio St. Andreas* sets six miles east-southeast. And yet another six miles from there live *Natureller* at another small river which, however, is not named on the charts. From that place the coast stretches for another twelve miles, of low land covered [46] by scrub and bush, to *Cuteru* or *Cuteru lahu* [Coetroe], where one sees "double forest," and immediately in front of that, out in the sea, there is a rock, both of which things are good landmarks for that town.[89]

From there to *Cabu lahu*, a distance of one and one-half miles, there is flat land, where the Tusk Coast ends; and for the purchase of tusks one uses iron rods, basins, bracelets of metal, knives, coarse cloth, white glass beads, small casks made of poor quality *manggods*, and large fish hooks; and then the *Quaqua Coast* begins, of which that same *Cabo lahu* is the most prominent place, where one is not forced to take the least trouble one's self to trade, since [47] the inhabitants immediately come aboard in great numbers, and are right good folk. Their wares are tusks and striped cotton cloth, along with the fruits of the land, chickens and wax; and one anchors there at fourteen or twelve fathoms.[90]

East of *Cabo lahu* one sees double land right to *Iaqve*, or *Tiebe-lahu*, which is also a trading place, and in like manner, there are also good folk there to deal with.[91] And the inhabitants from *Tiebe-lahu*, just as from the abovementioned *Cuteru*, usually come aboard if one just lies quietly at *Cabo lahu*, which is halfway between both these places, and one and one-half miles from each of them, [48] the one to the west and the other to the east.

The coast now stretches mostly easterly for sixteen miles, past *Wetu*, right to *Jeaqve*, or *Icaqveleaqve* [sic] where there is also a good trading place; and from there it is six miles to the deep hole, or abyss, where there is no bottom; yet another three miles from there, running in a northeasterly direction, there is a river called *Rio de Sveria de Costa*, which appears when one comes out of the west, and at its western bank there is a rock on the beach which stands quite dry on land, so that the water cannot wash over it, whose like one cannot find earlier along the coast, and next to this rock there is a [49] completely square bush, by which that river can easily be recognized.[92]

It is not possible to name all the landing places which the Blacks here on the *Qvaqva Coast* have, since they put in to land and out to sea wherever they please, and are well practiced and accustomed to the sea, in their way, so that they are first on the surface for an hour, and then underwater for an hour, which must be viewed by everyone who sees it with the greatest wonder.[93] Therefore, one has no need to specify and make special mention of every town and small trading place there, since, at all those places they come aboard willingly themselves, as has been stated before, when they see that one reduces sail and that one wants to trade.[94]

CHAPTER FIVE
Gold Coast[95]

From [50] the aforementioned *Rio de Sveria de Costa* the *Coast* stretches east by south by east-southeast for twelve miles to the first trading place on the *Gold Coast*, which is *Assené* [Assini], reckoned to lie twenty-eight miles from *Cabo lahu* on the *Qvaqva Coast*, when one sails in a direct line to that point and does not put in at every single trading place. One anchors at that town at fourteen and thirteen fathoms in good ground; and this is a good landmark, [that] when one comes along the *Coast*, to the west of the town there are two or three tall bushes and then one more which is very tall and thick, and when sailing past them one sights a number of palm trees which stand [51] separately from one another, the one tall, the other low, [that is] just where the town lies.

Several years ago the French had the intention of establishing a fort there, and when they saw a ship they flew a white flag on a pole at that place; however, nothing came of it.

There one finds very good gold, and the Blacks who live there are well versed in *negotien*, indeed, nearly as well so as the Christians; some of them speak a little Dutch, English, and Portuguese as well.[96]

The wares traded from the Christians to the Blacks, from *Assené* to *Tessie* [Teshi] are: *Say, Rask, Lerret,* bedsheets packed in chests, [52] cotton cloth of [*i. e.* such as] *Necanesser, Tapetanteinos, Pentades, Taffezeles,* blue *Baftas, Zitsen,* and other colorful East Indian cottons; likewise gunpowder, guns, all manner of glass beads, iron, brass pans, pewter plates, flintstone, tankards, padlocks, knives, fish hooks, bells, old reblocked hats, blood coral, tallow, and corn brandy. But, regarding other beverages, such as wine, *Sek, Momme, Lybsk Seebier,* and French brandy, these are bought by the Christians.

Two miles east of here lies another trading place called *Ebenny* or *Abenny* [Abiane], east of which there stands a large square bush on the beach, [53] by which it can easily be recognized; and the inhabitants at this place are good people and have unadulterated gold.

Another two miles eastward lies the town of *Tebu* or *Tabu* [Tobo], near which there is high land so that one can see it easily from the place before; and one anchors both at *Ebenny* and *Tabu* at fourteen and thirteen fathoms.

Next to this place lies *Cabo Apollonia,* which is reckoned to be thirty-three miles from *Cabo lahu*. One must not come closer in than fifteen fathoms since the ground is foul there. The land at this place is high and there can be seen three or four mountains which, in clear [54] weather one can see from *Assené*; and there, too, there are good folk, and good gold to be had.

At these four trading places, *Assené, Ebenny, Tabu,* and *Cabo Apollonia,* one can also, at times, get elephant tusks, just as on the *Tusk Coast,* yet they are not such a good buy; and one must always examine those tusks with a stick to see if there is stone or gravel inside them, which has been put in to increase their weight, which is often found, to the reduction [*sic*] of many pounds.

From this last trading place and to the first fort on the *Gold Coast* the land runs in a slight curve, and the course sets southeast for seven miles, [55] where one finds good anchoring ground at fourteen or fifteen fathoms.

This fortress, or fort, is called *Aximb* [Fort St. Anthony] and was first built by the Portuguese, who called it *Appam* at that time. But in the year 1642, on 9 February, it was taken from them by force by the Dutch, who still have it in their possession.

It lies on a slight rise near the sea, and in fine weather is clearly visible for those who come from the west, until one is nearly there, when it is hidden from sight by a cliff which lies in front of it. It is equipped with thirty-six cannons, twenty-eight common soldiers, a chief merchant, [56] a sub-merchant, twenty *assistants,* a *sergeant,* twenty *Gefriedere,* a barber, a constable, and a drummer. The *Negeri* [African settlement], or town which lies under this fort can muster three hundred men with guns, when necessary.

At this same fort there is a most excellent garden with oranges, pomegranates, *cassu,* pineapples, bananas, *water-limon-*

er, plantains, coconuts, and small citrons in abundance, which fruits they do not bother to save for any newly-arrived ship from the North which wants to anchor here.

There is much good gold here and the trade must be carried on mostly at night so the [57] *Company's* [Dutch West India Company] revenue officers may know nothing about it, since the Dutch have imposed a strict prohibition against trading anywhere along the *Coast* with *particuliere* ships.

Three miles south-southeast of there lie three points of land which extend into the sea, which are called *Cabo tres Puntas* [*Cape Three Points*], where the Brandenburgers, in the year 1682 established a fort called *Great Friderichs-Berg*, equipped with thirty cannons, sixty common soldiers, a *Director-Governor*, a chief merchant, a sub-merchant, three assistants, a *lieutenant*, a *Fendrich*, two *sergeants*, two *corporals*, a chief and sub-barber, a *constable*, some *volunteers* or *Adels-Burser*, and a *drummer*.

[58] With the *Director-Governor's* permission they trade at that place without discrimination with whomever they choose, if they themselves [i. e., the Brandenburgers] have no ship in the road. Their *Negeri* [Pokesu] numbers one hundred and thirty men who are mostly deserters who have left other forts and settled down here.

The fort lies at 4 deg. 10 min. and can be seen far out to sea; one anchors at twenty-four fathoms in good ground right close to its eastern edge, and one can also get good water here with little trouble, if necessary.

A little east of here lies a lodge called *Accoda* [Akwida], established and well-built by the Dutch a few years ago, which [59] at first always made trouble both in trade and in other ways for the Brandenburgers, who, during a banquet a few years ago, cunningly invaded and conquered it, and they are still in possession of it today, according to the agreement made about it in Holland with the Brandenburgers. It is equipped with eight or ten small cannons and there are also a sub-merchant, a corporal, a *constable,* and twelve common soldiers. One can also get good gold there, when it is for sale.[97]

Two miles even farther east lies a large town called *Botteru* [Butri], where the Dutch, at times, have their people staying for trade in a packhouse, which is like a [60] a small *lodge,* but without cannons; and there one must examine the gold well, since it is false at times.[98]

Four miles from here, to the east, the *Anteen* reef runs out into the sea, and right close to its western side there is another small trading place, *Attreba,* and one must not stand in closer to that reef than at 14, 13, and 12 fathoms, and to the other previously named places, *Accoda* and *Botteru,* at 15 and 14 fathoms in good ground.[99] Here, too, the gold is not of the best, and must be well examined and tested.

A little east of that reef of *Anteen* lies another trading place, *Takorary* [Takoradi], which formerly belonged to the Danes, [61] and at that same town, a half mile out to sea, there is a large rock, where one can see the surf breaking on it as a warning; and at times the Dutch and English also have their people staying there in small lodges in order to trade among the *Natureller.* The gold here is absolutely poor and is called *kakara* gold; and one anchors here, when one has the town to the west-northwest, in eight fathoms of water in good ground.[100]

Farther eastward there is still another trading place and lodge called *Secondé* [Secondi], equipped by the English with eight small cannons, a merchant, and eight common soldiers; and the Dutch, likewise, have their people staying [there] for the trade at times; [62] like the English; and the gold here is like that of the place before.[101]

From here the *Coast* stretches northeast by east for three miles and then the land forms a bay for about a mile farther, to *Samma* [Shama], where a river runs out from land, from which ships often take water. This *lodge, Samma,* belongs to the Dutch and is equipped with twelve small cannons, a merchant, two *assistants,* and twelve common soldiers; and one anchors east-southeast of there at 6, 7, and 8 fathoms of water in good ground.

From *Samma* the *Coast* stretches southeast by east again for a distance of two miles, as far as a round hill which lies at the edge of the sea, and [63] immediately east of that point there is a trading place called *Little Commendo* [Little Komenda], where one anchors at 6 and six and one-half fathoms of water, such that one has the abovementioned hill in the northwest by west, and then it is another three miles to *St. George d'el Mina.*

A half mile from this same *Little Commendo* lies another trading place called *Great Commendo,* at which there is also a hill, where a few years ago the English and Dutch established two *fortresses,* the one right close to the other, and each of them was equipped with sixteen cannons and [a staff of] twenty men, of high and low status, besides their slaves. And the *Natureller* [64] who live around here are all well-practiced in the use of handguns and have little or no fear of gunpowder and charge.[102] However, regarding the gold trade here, one must by all means pay close attention at both of these places, since the inhabitants trade openly with adulterated gold, weighted to four, five, or six *rixdalers,* by which many a one has been cheated.

Between *Great Commendo* and *St. George d'el Mina* there is a single small town, *Terre Peckenina* or *Peckinha,* from which there is a reef stretching all the way to *d'el Mina,* yet it is largely close to land so no seafarer need have any fear of it.[103]

When one has sailed past this reef one [65] comes to the aforementioned *St. George d'el Mina* [Elmina], which is the chief castle of the Dutch and the largest on the entire *Coast,* equipped with fifty large cannons, and a moat has been made in the hard rock around it.[104]

There is a *civilian* staff made up of a *Director-General* over all the trade in the entire land, a chief *commissioner* or merchant, a *fiscal,* a *general* bookkeeper in charge of the books, an *Equipage-Mester,* a priest, an assistant merchant, eight *assistants,* a hospital superintendent, a *magasin-mester,* a chief barber and an assistant, and a *Forlœsere*; and the *military* staff consists of an officer-in-chief, two *constables,* two *sergeants,* three [66] corporals, twelve *Adels-Burser,* two drummers, and one hundred and fifty common soldiers who are used for various purposes, and a *Profos.* This is the complete garrison, besides which there are *Mulattoes,* or the children of Christian men bred from the black women, and other servants from among the slaves and *Natureller* of the place.

The castle was built by the Portuguese in the year 1481 when their *Admiral Diego Zabuya* [d'Azambuja] was on the Coast with thirteen battle ships, in the service of the king of Portugal, John the Second, to seek trade with the inhabitants; at which time, in the kingdom of *Fetu* where the castle lies the ruler was *Carramanasse,* who first allowed the Christians to build *lodges* in that land.[105]

[**67**] But after the aforementioned Portuguese had had this fort for many years, and had fortified it well and provided it with everything, they began to behave very unjustly to the inhabitants and, finally, tyrannized them severely. Meanwhile, the Dutch had also begun to trade on the *Coast* with their ships, and upon their application the *Natureller* were more than willing to give the Dutch permission to drive out the Portuguese, who were now their enemies. Whereupon an attempt was made then and there on that castle, in the year 1637, and it was taken by the Dutch, and the Portuguese were entirely driven out of the land, after having had the trade there quite to themselves since the year 1481.[106]

[**68**] The seizure of that castle was greatly aided by the existence of a hill which lies close by, where there is now a very strong fort, of which, however, nothing can be reported since no stranger is allowed to visit it; and the hill and the fort are both called *St. Jago* because the *Castle d'el Mina*, with the help of that hill, was taken on *St. Jacob's Day.*[107]

The river which runs through the entire *Fetu* kingdom empties into the sea just at the castle, providing both forts with great means of defense on their eastern side; furthermore, at this place one has the largest *Negeri* to be found at the seaside on the entire Coast, called *Amppeny,* which [**69**] can muster some thousand men in the event of war, all with guns and well-trained.[108] And one can anchor east of *d'el Mina* at 6, 7, and 8 fathoms with good sand ground, where one has an unimpeded view of *Fort St. Jago* lying to the east, and a good view of the land between them.

One and one-half miles east-southeast of here lies the English chief castle *Cabo Corsso* [Cape Coast], equipped with fifty-four cannons, a *Director-Governor* in charge of the entire trade, a chief merchant, a priest, two assistant merchants, a vice-bookkeeper, a chief officer, a *Magasin-Mester,* four assistants, two barbers, [**70**] two sergeants, three constables, three corporals, six *Adels-Burser,* two drummers, eighty common soldiers, and two *Profosser,* as well as the *Mulattoes,* slaves, and the Natureller [who are] servants of the Christians.¹⁰⁹

Many changes have taken place at that castle since it was first built in the year 1652 by the Swedes, with the permission of the king in the country; it was then called *Carolus-Berg,* and the cornerstone was laid by a Governor Isaac Melville, born in Basel in Switzerland.¹¹⁰ But in the year 1658 it was taken from the Swedes by a Swede named *Henrich Carlof* and handed over to the Danes, at which time a man by [71] the name of *Samuel Schmidt* was appointed governor there; in the year 1659, in the month of April, along with the two *lodges Takorary* and *Anemobu* [Anomabu], as well as the *lodge* at *Ursoe* [Osu], it was again given over to the Dutch in a traitorous manner upon the payment of a great amount of money, who, however, did not keep it long.¹¹¹ During that same month of April it was taken away from them by the *Natureller* and again committed to the Swedes, who, thereupon, appointed a governor by the name of *Anthonie Vos* from Hamburg, who governed it very well until the year 1663, when the *Natureller* took it away from the Swedes again, with cunning, and, in return for large payments delivered it to the Dutch.¹¹²

[72] At that time the Dutch were virtual masters of the entire *Coast* and did not, in any way, want to permit any other nation to be found in that area; therefore, from *Cabo Corsso* they began to fire on the Danish *Castle Friderichs-Berg* [Fredriksborg] which lies close by, seized the Danish lodge near *Cabo Corsso* on 23 March 1664, and treated the Danes who were stationed there wretchedly; and with great diligence prepared to storm *Friderichsberg,* so that the garrison there was in greatest danger both night and day, until GOD unexpectedly sent some help, in that on 14 April the same year the English *Admiral* [Captain] *Robert Holms* [73] arrived to anchor in the road there with thirteen capital ships, and informed the Danes on that same day that the King of Denmark and the King of England had formed an alliance, and that he had orders to *assist* the Danes there in every way as far as possible, which orders were immediately executed ¹¹³ Consequently the Danes and the English, in return for the presentation of some gifts, were given permission by the *Fetus*

to *attack* the Dutch at their discretion; whereupon, with great difficulty, a number of large cannons were brought up to *Friderichsberg* as soon as possible, and *Cabo Corsso* was immediately fired upon, both from land and sea, but the heaviest and most steadfast was from *Friderichsberg*; which continued [**74**] thus for eight days and nights without stop before the Dutch *Governor Tobias Pensado*, who was a Frenchman, gave up the fort by contract, so that on the following 3 May it came into English hands, where it still is today.

Under the fort there is a fairly large *Negeri* called *Ugva* [Ogua], inhabited largely by fishermen, therefore it cannot muster more than four hundred men with guns; and one can anchor there, east of the fort in 7 fathoms of sandy ground.[114]

A cannon-shot east of here lies the aforementioned Danish chief castle *Friderichsberg*, which was established in the year 1659 [**75**] by the Danish *Governor Joseph Kramer*.[115] But in the year 1685, on 16 April, it was, without any orders and contrary to all reason, handed over as a mortgage payment by *Governor Hans Lykke* to the English at *Cabo Corsso*, who still have it in their possession, and in this way it was lost to the Danish *chartered* Company.

It was built on a hill three hundred paces high and was, earlier, equipped with twenty-three cannons, a governor, a chief merchant, an assistant merchant, a priest, a lieutenant, a barber, two *assistants*, a *sergeant*, a *constable*, two corporals, six *Adelsburser*, a drummer and [**76**] twenty – eight common soldiers. But at present there are no more than twelve common soldiers there, with a junior officer and a constable, since there is hardly any trade there, and it is held in *possession* purely as a place from which *Cabo Corsso* was won earlier and still can be won easily, in the same manner as *St. Jago* at *d'el Mina*, as described earlier.[116]

Under the fort there are five small *Negerier*, separate from one another, but mostly in ruins at present; and at the fort there are two gardens with fruit whose equal cannot be found on the entire *Coast*, except at *Aximb*, which has been mentioned earlier.[117]

[**77**] The mountain that the fort is on is called *Amamforé* in the language of the country, and it is the last fort in the *Fetu* kingdom, which begins at Commando [sic] and ends a half *fjerding*'s

distance to the east of this fort, at a small bay called *Amacrofu;* so that that kingdom borders on the open sea to the south, on the kingdom *Abrahambu* [Abrem] to the north, on *Commendo* to the west, and on the kingdom *Sabu* [Asebu] to the east, and it is barely three miles in breadth and a good six miles in length.[118]

The three main castles touched upon before, namely *St. George d'el Mina, Cabo Corsso,* and *Friderichsberg,* were established in [78] this kingdom of *Fetu* because the inhabitants were found to be much more decent in every way than their neighbors; for which reason this kingdom always flourished more than the others with good trade, and this continued for a long time, but due to wars of long duration it is now quite in ruins.[119]

From *Friderichsberg* and the aforementioned mountain *Amamforé* on which the fort lies, to the east, at a distance of one *fjerding* there is a town called *Kong* [Mt. Cong], inhabited mostly by fishermen, where the kingdom of *Sabu* begins. This is on a high hill, so that in clear weather one can see eleven Christian forts and *lodges* from there, namely in the west two at *Commendo* [79] which belong to the English and Dutch; *St. George d'el Mina, St. Jago, Cabo Corsso,* and *Friderichsberg;* and to the east there are *Fort Nassow, Ennechiannus, Mannemobu, Agia,* and *Cormantyn,* descriptions of which now follow.

At that same *Kong* there is always a Dutch person staying in a small house, to engage in a little trade with the inhabitants, as well as to be on the lookout for newly-arrived ships, since from there one can see them far out to sea.[120]

Yet another good *fjerding's* distance farther to the east lies the Dutch *Fortress Nassow,* equipped with twenty-two cannons, a chief merchant, an assistant merchant, two *assistants,* [80] a barber, a sergeant, a corporal, a constable, four *Adels-Burser,* a drummer, and twenty common soldiers, as well as the *Natureller,* and this *fortress* is the only one in the *Sabu* kingdom and one of the oldest on the Coast, and it is very well made but absolutely unhealthful.[121] Under it lies a *Negeri* called *Mourée* [Mori], inhabited mostly by fishermen, so it cannot muster more than a hundred men with guns. And the gold here must be examined with great care. It is also necessary to take care, when one wants to anchor at *Mourée* or to seek trade there that one anchors just between it and *Ennechianus,* which comes next, at 8, 7, and 6 fathoms in good ground, where one will see the canoes come out immediately.[122]

[81] *Ennechiang* lies at a distance of one and one-half *fjerding* from *Fort Nassow* and *Mourée* and is an English *lodge,* which formerly was a small fortress, where there is a merchant, an assistant, a corporal, and six common soldiers, as well as the *Natureller,* and the cannons found there now are only four small one-pounders. The kingdom of *Fantijn* begins here, where the gold is found to be much adulterated.[123]

A short mile from here, eastwards, lies the aforementioned former Danish *lodge,* which is now a fortress, *Manomobu,* called *Anomobu* [Anomabu] by the inhabitants, which is now in the possession of the English, who acquired it along with *Cabo Corsso,* and it is equipped [82] with twelve cannons, as well as some small ones of no value, a chief merchant, an assistant merchant, an *assistant,* a constable, a corporal, and eight common soldiers, and there is only a small *Negeri* near it.[124]

One anchors just in front of the fort at six fathoms in good ground, where one can see *Cormantin* to the east by south and three high mountains inland, separated from one another in such a way that one can see between all three.

The land around here forms a bay which begins at *Cabo Corsso* and ends at *Cormantin,* so that the course from *Cabo Corsso* to *Mourée* is east by north and then again east by south, to [83] *Cormantin,* as noted before; and this fort must lie north by west of the ship when one anchors at *Mourée.*

At a distance of a half *fjerding* from there lies another English *lodge* called *Agia* [Egya], and *Adra* by some, where there are stationed six Christians, but without cannons, and there is nothing of value there.[125]

Outside the aforementioned bay, on a mountain, lies the Dutch *Fortress Cormantin* where one anchors directly in front of the *Negeri,* at seven fathoms in good ground. It is provided with twenty-four cannons, a chief merchant, an assistant merchant, two *assistants,* a barber, a sergeant, a corporal, [84] four *Adels-Burser,* a constable, a drummer, and twenty common soldiers, as well as the *Natureller;* and the *Negeri* can muster three hundred men with guns.[126]

This fort lies at almost the same height as the aforementioned *Friderichsberg,* and was taken from the English by *Admiral Ruyter,* and there is much poor gold to be had, where one can easily be cheated if he is not familiar with it.[127]

Six miles east by south of here there is a mountain called *Duyvelsberg,* or Devil's Mountain, where the Evil Spirit always rules, and indulges in so much haunting that it cannot be described, indeed, it is quite unbelievable. It slopes right down to the shore, and can [85] be seen four miles out to sea; and between *Cormantin* and it [i.e. the mountain] there are four small fishing towns, which one can clearly see [separately], the one from the other.[128]

From this mountain the course sets east by north for five miles to *Breku* [Senya Beraku], where the English, according to reports, have recently established a small fort where they have used the cannons which formerly were at *Friderichsberg*; and they have manned it with eighteen Christian persons of both high and low status.[129]

The town lies nearly a half *fjerding* inland in a large thicket of trees and bushes on a mountain, and it is usually a good place for trading, and there are good [86] people there, and close to the *Negeri* there is a single tree, just as on the coast at *Dorryn,* by which the place is easily recognized.[130]

The *Qvambus* assert that the kingdom of *Acara* starts here, which, however, is incorrect, and [they state] this purely to be able to have *Breku* under their yoke, as well as all the other free *Negerier* around there, against whom they have often exercised the greatest violence and treated them improperly.[131]

After this place the course is five miles east-northeast to *Wimba* [Winneba] where, earlier, there was a *lodge* which was ruined by the *Qvambus,* and there is no significant trade there.[132]

[87] Somewhat farther to the east one can see a small mount called *Kock's Bröd* [Cock's Loaf/Dampa Hill], at which, when all things are considered justly, the kingdom of *Acara* begins, according to the *Naturellernes* own conviction.[133] But, as far as it

is in their power, as mentioned before, the *Qvambus* consider it part of their kingdom.

CHAPTER SIX
Acara [*Accra*][134]

When one has passed *Kocks-Brød* one will see land that is lower than that seen before, for from this mountain and back to the west, as reported before, one sees nothing along that high coast but mountains and high banks, intermingled everywhere. But from this same mountain eastward the land is found to be quite flat at the shore for two [88] or three miles, with some coconut trees growing there; which trees, growing at the shore without fruit, are called the *Spanish Cavalry*; and above them, farther inland, some mountains are visible, yet they are in no way comparable to those described earlier.[135]

As soon as one has passed the so-called *Spanish Cavalry* one can clearly see the three Christian fortresses situated in that same kingdom, *Acara*; the first one, belonging to the English, is called *James Castle* or *Jacob's Fort*, equipped with twenty-eight large and small cannons, a chief merchant [89] an assistant, a barber, a sergeant, a constable, a drummer, and twenty common soldiers, as well as the Christians' servants and some slaves. The *Negeri* here is called *Sioco* [Sokko/Soco/Tshoco], which cannot muster more than sixty men with guns.[136]

At a cannon-shot from here, eastward, lies the Dutch *fortress* called *Creve-Coeur*, which is the largest of all three situated here. It is equipped with twenty-eight cannons, a chief and an assistant merchant, two *assistants,* a barber, a sergeant, a corporal, three *Adelsburser,* a drummer, and twenty-four common soldiers, as well as their slaves and *Naturellen* as servants; and in the year 1692, by decree of [90] Nicolaus Sweru, General Director at *St. George d'el Mina*, an excellent warehouse, with lodgings for the merchant, was very well built of Dutch materials. Under the fort lies the *Negeri Aprag* [Little Accra], which can muster a good five hundred men with guns.[137]

Still another cannon-shot east of here lies the Danish *Fortress Christiansburg*, equipped with twenty-eight cannons, a vice commander, an assistant merchant, a priest, a barber, three *as-*

sistants, a sergeant, a corporal, a constable, three *Adelsburser* or *Gefriedere,* a drummer, and twenty-six common soldiers.[138]

This fort was, at the very beginning, [91] a small *lodge* built in the year 1650, and then on the orders of the Danish governor at *Friderichsberg, Henning Albrecht,* improved in the year 1659 and made into a fortress, for the most part in the form in which it now exists.[139] Yet it was not brought to *perfection* before the now late *Christen Cornelissøn* (who had formerly served the Swedes there for a period of seven years) came to that fort to be the chief merchant on behalf of the Danish Company in the year 1661, when he had the walls rebuilt from the ground up, and brought to completion all aspects of the *fortification,* which had only been laid out beforehand.

[92] And yet, because of his good *conduct,* fidelity, and industriousness, he was envied both secretly and openly to the highest degree by his enemies there (of whom he had no lack to the day of his death) so that, at times, he was close to being murdered had he not been wonderfully protected by GOD and, indeed, by the support of the *Natureller;* yet he served the Company at that fort with the utmost fidelity for six years, and at the same time helped greatly to build up the trade. He was so respected by the Natives, both the mightiest as well as the lowliest for his friendly manner and good relationships that when he [93] had orders to leave there and return to the Fatherland, the king of *Acara* himself,[140] with all his queens and his entire council, came farther down into the country and towards the sea coast than he had ever been before (since no king, according to the customs of the land, and without the intervention of their *Fitissies,* is permitted to come from the town where he lives as far as to the sea coast) and this, alone, in order to take leave of him [*Cornelissøn*]; the king complaining bitterly that not only was *Cornelissøn* going to leave them but that he himself was so wretched at not being able to accompany him to the shore himself, therefore he ordered his queens, his council [94] and musicians to accompany him there, which was done, yet not without great expense, because of the gifts which had to be distributed to each of them for such a show of honor. Indeed not only is he still, today, highly eulogized by the *Natureller,* but his name will not die out so soon among

them, either, since many of them, in his memory, have named their children after him, calling them *Cornelissi,* so that after his departure and death they had, and still have, in the *Acara* kingdom, many *Christen Cornelissi* in the place where they only had one when he lived among them. This, briefly, that his illustrious posthumous reputation be remembered.[141]

[95] In the year 1579 the fort was given up and delivered to the Portuguese for thirty-six pounds of gold, in a traitorous manner by the merchant *Peiter* [sic] *Bolt,* who was in command there at that time; but in the year 1683, on 26 February, it came into Danish hands again, after the Portuguese, on strict orders from their king, quietly and without telling anyone, had left it and gone away.[142]

After that, in the year 1691, in the month of January, by the [Danish] king's most gracious will and desire, it was placed under the direction of one of his Royal Majesty of Denmark's *Commercie-Raad,* the honorable *Nicolaus Janssen Arf.* [96] improved everywhere and provided with all the necessities;[143] but in the year 1693, in the month of June, it was occupied by the *Qvambus* with the permission of their *King Barsiar* [Bassua], the Christians staying there were badly treated and the funds of the abovementioned Mr. *Commercie-Raad* which were found there, and which made up a large sum, were taken away; which [fort] was held by them for an entire year, until the month of June in the following year, 1694, when (although for the payment to the *Qvambus* of a large sum of money) it again came under the direction of the abovementioned Mr. *Commercie-Raad,* under whom it still is today.[144]

[97] Near the fort lies a *Negeri* called *Ursow* [Osu], which can muster three hundred men with guns for war; and when one wants to anchor there one should sail a little beyond the fort, eastward, and drop anchor in six and one-half fathoms of water, in very foul ground so that the anchor must be weighed every day if one does not want to lose it; and the harbor there is also very poor for landing, so that Christians have often damaged both life and goods when they have tried to land there.[145]

Half a mile east of here, to the north, lies a large town called *Labbadé* [Labadi], where a tall tree stands at its southern side, making a good [98] landmark for the town. But if one wants to trade here one must sail past it with shortened sails, right to *Tessie* [Teshi], which lies a half-mile to the east, where one should drop anchor just in front of that town and remain for a night and a day before weighing anchor again, since the *Qvambus* often buy many goods here through the merchants who live in *Labbadé*, for which they must have some time.[146]

The *Gold Coast* and the kingdom of *Acara* end at this town of *Tessie*, although they now consider it to extend another mile farther, to a small fishing town called *Nungo* [Nungua], which will be described later.

This, then, is a short but sufficiently detailed description of the trading places [99] and the correct names of the forts and ports of call along the entire Coast where there is anything to be undertaken; since, from *Tessie*, east by north and east-northeast there is *daabelt Land* for a distance of twelve miles, inhabited mostly by fishermen, to *Rio de Volta*, which goes right to *Arder* [Allada] where the slave trade begins, but that is another matter which shall be treated later. Since the Danish *Fort Christiansburg* is located in the *Acara* kingdom, and the Danes, at present, carry on most of their trade there, I shall first, and before I leave the Gold Coast, write a little about that kingdom in particular, as well as about the gold there and on the entire *Gold Coast*, [100] after which I shall write briefly about the aforementioned slave trade, and then something about a number of things in the entire *Guinea* area in general, such as: about the inhabitants' superstition and idolatry, the fruits of the land, domestic and wild animals, birds, fish, and reptiles, as well as which wares are traded there, and other things that might be useful to know and observe.

CHAPTER SEVEN
About the Kingdom *Acara*

This kingdom, *Acara*, which rightly has its beginning in the west at the mountain *Kocks-Brød* and ends in the east at the town of *Tessie*, has, since a score of years ago, expanded five miles farther west, [**101**] that is, to *Breku,* and a mile farther east to *Nungo,* as mentioned before, thus, instead of, as formerly, having been only six miles from east to west, it is now twelve miles, and seven miles from south to north; and the country itself is reckoned to be the best to be found on the entire Coast along the shore, from *Cabo Verde* to this point.[147]

In the same kingdom lie the aforementioned Christian forts, *James Castle, Creve-Coeur,* and *Christiansburg,* each of which makes a monthly payment to the king there of thirty-two *rixdaler,* all together ninety-six *rixdaler,* which is called *custom*;[148] besides a certain amount to the highest-ranking *Negroes* or [**102**] *Cabusees,* who live close to the forts and who are paid individually by each nation in these forts.[149]

The city [*Stad*] *Qvambu*[150], which is now considered to be the capital of that kingdom [*Accra*], is a good three miles inland from the shore, and, by pacing, which I myself have tried and measured, I reckon it to be two miles long but only one hundred and sixty feet wide; so that it consists only of a single street which stretches out in a line so straight that it could have been laid out along a string, with houses built on both sides. Although it is now considered to be the capital of that kingdom, yet it is is not so by right, [**103**] but had formerly to *contribute* and pay taxes to the king of this kingdom [*Acara*] until the year 1677 when its inhabitants, with the aid and support of others, rose up and waged war against him, who was then killed, and the proper capital, *Acara* [Great Accra], which was very large and very well built, according to the manner of the land, was *ruined* by them and finally totally burned to the ground, whose walls and half the road to Qvambu can still be clearly seen.[151]

That same revolt did not end without becoming the greatest war in a number of years, during which [period] the *fortresses* suffered great need, and the English and the Dutch had to concede everything the *Qvambus* [**104**] desired, in which they were unsuccessful among the Danes in that what they got there were blows instead of booty, and they had to *retreat* voluntarily.[152]

Their leader at that time was a very large, fat and tall *Negro* by the name of *Rensang Sasaraku* [Ansa Sasraku], who was *Prince Ado's* father, and who died immediately the war ended.[153] [He was then] King of *Acara* and *Qvambu,* which he had united by the sword; but after his death his government was placed in the hands of his *Brafu* (which is comparable to his field marshal) by the name of *Bansiar* [Basua], until *Prince Ado* would come of age; and although he [the prince] has long since reached the age when he could [**105**] assume the government, yet his subjects have not been willing to offend the aforementioned *Bansiar* because of his great old age, so the prince will not take over the government until after his death.[154]

Since that time the *Qvambus* and their chief and king have governed the kingdom, although compared to their predecessors who had ruled there they are nothing but coarse peasants and foolish people, in the opinion of the other Blacks on the coast; but they dare not let this opinion be known.[155]

Both live in that town of *Qvambu, King Bansiar* nearly [**106**] in the middle of it, and *Prince Ado* a good half-mile north-northwest of him, with many other free *Negroes* and their slaves. Both the king's house and that of the prince are in the middle of the street, between the rows of houses on each side. And it is reckoned that the town can muster seven thousand men, provided they have the help of the twenty-two large and small *Negerier* which lie in that kingdom.[156]

The king has six rights by which he is acknowledged to be their chief and the most superior among them:

The first is the collection of the above mentioned monthly customs, as well as other small gifts [**107**] given, at times, by the three Christian fortresses in the kingdom.[157]

The second is that he himself judges all the cases which occur among the *Natureiler,* which usually do not come up among the poor but mostly among the rich, who do not easily go free without large payments, as long as they are unwilling to lose their heads.

The third is that he enjoys a portion of the country's produce after the annual harvest, from all who live everywhere in the country, not so much for the sake of the value of the produce as for the proof that they owe submission to him.[158]

The fourth is that there is no felling of game, such as [108] buffalo, elephants, tigers, leopards or others, without his enjoying his part of each.[159]

The fifth is that the best plantations in *Qvambu* belong to him.[160]

The sixth is that he has for warfare the best and most experienced slaves to be found in the entire country.[161]

And, although *Prince Ado* and his *Cabusees* can muster many more people than the king, yet they are not as experienced as the king's, and they are all together coarse peasants, so that he who understands their language hears, with greatest astonishment, their ideas about various things; apart from the roguery and violence in which they are well trained [109] and which they are taught more of daily by a number of *Negroes* who had served many years ago at the coast, both in the *fortresses* and in the Negerier, and then among those living in *Qvambu*.[162]

The inhabitants in the kingdom have six chief ways of making a living; the first is by fishing; the second is to make salt; the third is the cultivation of the earth with grain and fruit; the fourth is animal husbandry and sale; the fifth is to *negotiate* with the Christians on behalf of other *Negroes* who do not themselves understand *negotien* or are unable to speak to those Christians; and the sixth is by making war.[163] And even though there are in that kingdom [110] those *Negroes* who work with iron and gold, as well as those who practice hunting, yet they cannot be included in the list above.[164] Thus:

1. The fish that is caught here, and most of it is caught in October, is sold yearly for a great deal of money after it

has been dried. It is called *Pargos,* is as large as a good bream, and is carried many miles inland, from one hand to another, so that this is a source of great trade.[165]

2. Regarding salt, which is made at *Labbade, Tessie, Ursow,* as well as at the coconut trees which are called the *Spanish Cavalry,* and some at *Nungo,* it is, in the same way, [111] bought by the inhabitants living here and there in the land and carried from the one to the other, very far inland as an article of trade.[166]

3. Regarding cultivation of the earth with all the varieties of the country's fruits and grain, it is carried on mostly at the capital *Qvambu,* from which place it is transported to the *Negerier* on the coast and traded in great quantities for salt and fish, besides being sold daily for money to anyone who wants it.[167]

4. The raising of animals such as oxen and sheep for trade is not practised in the kingdom by ordinary people but largely by the most prominent, or *Cabusees,* who live [112] under the forts because it is an expensive undertaking, since for a small ox one must pay thirty-four *rixdaler,* and for a good, fat sheep eight *rixdaler.* They are purchased in the first place mostly from *Arder* [Allada] and the slave places as very thin, but then, in this grassy land, they are so well nourished that in a period of fourteen days they can become quite fat.[168]

5. Regarding trade *negotien,* this is not carried on by everyone or by others than those who understand it and can speak the country's Portuguese, as well as having a knowledge of weights; they are, for the most part, *Cabusees* at the forts and those *Negroes* who have been in the service of the Christians earlier. Those *Natureller* [113] who are used for this service know very well how to cheat the peasants and those who are strangers to the country and who are not at all acquainted with trade negotiation, but must believe whatever they are told and presented to them, in the manner of the country.[169]

To wage war and let one's self be used thus is absolutely the custom in this kingdom, and it occurs most after *travat* times, in the months of June and July here, when the fruits begin to ripen, so that they have food everywhere.[170] Thus, as soon as anyone, after a simple report or in some other way, suspects that he or one of his people has been wronged or suffered an injustice, be it a short time ago or many years before, and he can revenge it in some way without letting the *Qvambu* government hear of it, he goes to work on it, both day and night, continuing in one way or another [114] until he has at last satisfied his will. But if the conditions of the case are of such importance that it should be brought before the *Qvambu* authorities, those same *Qvambus* buy the case themselves, and, later, in their way, given the time and opportunity, they very cunningly and roguishly wage war against the one who feels himself most secure and free of all danger; so there is hardly ever any peace among *Naturellerne* in the vicinity and the poor people who are outside the kingdom.[171] And when the *Qvambus,* on oath or by their fetish or faith, elaborately declare that they will wage war in the east, then it is usually done in the west; so that no one who does not know their ways should believe them too strongly, since no good manners or [sense of] right of any kind can be found among them. And they are nothing but coarse peasants who support themselves mostly by the cultivation of the earth and its fruits, by the work of their slaves.[172]

[115] And if this is found to be a somewhat brief report of the kingdom *Acara,* there now follows a little more.

CHAPTER EIGHT

About the gold on the *Gold Coast* and other places in the land

The *Gold Coast* is considered [to extend] from *Assené* to *Nungo*, which, in a straight line, is a distance of 100 and ten [*sic*] miles, where one receives mostly gold for the wares brought from Europe. Yet, that gold is not found everywhere on this coast, even though it is called *Gold Coast,* but it comes from a good thirty miles inland from the shore, and mostly from the kingdom of *Acania* [*Accany/Akany/Akani*], which is held to be the largest kingdom in Guinea, stretching in length east-north-east to south-southwest a distance of ninety miles.[173]

This gold is not brought by the *Acanies* directly to the Christians but to the *Natureller* in the neighboring [116] kingdoms of *Acara, Fantyn, Sabu, Fetu, Adumb* [*Adom*], and other small provinces at the coast, and that gold is clean and pure without any adulteration at all.[174]

It is dug out of the earth by the *Acanies'* slaves entirely clean and pure, mostly as small particles of dust like fine sand, in which, at times, there are found some large nuggets worth 2, 3, 4, 5, 6, 7, and 8 Danish marks, indeed to a value of many *rixdaler,* but that is rare;[175] and the earth is not examined when it is dug up to see if it contains gold or not, but that same earth is placed by the slaves in large wooden bowls which they then carry to the nearest water in the area, where it is thrown down until a very large pile has been collected; and as soon as their superior, who is called *Bomba,* thinks the pile is large enough, they stop their digging and immediately other, flat wooden [117] basins are [made] ready, into which the slaves put the aforementioned collected earth, which, due to the sun's heat is quite dry and crisp and can therefore be dissolved immediately in the water and separated, which [the slaves] then take into the water and flush the water around in the basins so that all the earth floats out of them; by this process the very smallest grain of gold which is contained in it cannot be lost because of its weight, but sinks to the bottom. They continue with this until there is no more that floats and can be separated out, when gold and small stones and other heavy gravel which are found with it are left lying in the basins; yet this is not examined by the slaves to see if there is much or little gold among [the stones], but when their time to eat has come they carry all their basins to their abovementioned *Bomba*, and superior, who takes out of them everything to be found there, and using a copper sieve, as well as [118] some small basins called "blowing-basins" mostly by breathing and blowing with his mouth, he very adroitly separates them from one another so that the gold alone, which cannot be blown away, remains in the basin and all the impurities are blown away.[176]

In this way gold is found and exchanged from hand to hand, finally coming to the Christians on the coast. And indeed gold is often sought in the same way, by using slaves, in the kingdoms of *Fetu, Sabu,* and *Commendo* during rainy season, so that one can see several hundred of them standing close to the shore and rinsing earth from their basins, yet in the evening all they have for their entire day's work is of no value, for which reason it is not sought much there and most of it comes from no other place than from the aforementioned *Acania,* and from the small kingdoms scattered around the country which are under its jurisdiction and power.[177]

[119] The *Acanies,* with permission of the Christians, have their own merchants living at the main *castles St. George d'el Mina, Cabo Corsso,* and *Friderichsberg,* who understand the *Acania* language and can trade on their behalf, but not in the kingdom of *Acara:*[178] Since whatever they want to get from the Christians they must buy through the *Qvambus* who do not permit any *Acanies* to go through the kingdom of *Acara* to the coast in order to negotiate personally;[179] which right all of the other kings at the shore claim and, for the most part, have achieved; furthermore, they do it for the sake of cheating with the gold which has come to them in an unadulterated state so they can themselves adulterate it, and indulge in other such activities.[180]

Meanwhile, at present the Christians all along the *Coast* purchase at a gold price of one *Lod* of gold for eight *rixdaler* and sell for the same, so that whatever profit they make [120] is only on the wares which are sold for that gold. This is because every single *Negro, Cabusee, Marckedor,* or merchant, knows just as well how to deal with weights, as does the shrewdest Christian, indeed he can, by weighing it in his hand, distinguish a *Banco* weight from a true or troy weight.[181]

One can, with great care, and using the country's weights, divide the value of one *rixdaler* worth of this gold dust into twenty-four equal parts, which is done by using some small plants that resemble field peas, are quite red and are called *Dambar,* which grow wild everywhere in the country; and twenty-four of them of equal size are chosen to make up one *rixdaler* of gold. There also grow some other varieties of peas, but not wild, called *Taku,* which are larger and quite white with a black dot on the end, of which twelve are calculated to equal one *rixdaler;* these *Dambarer* and *Takuner* are used daily by everyone on [121] the *Gold Coast,* since all the servants of the Christians receive their salaries and wages in gold, and must in turn pay the *Natureller* for fish, chickens, eggs, fruit, bread, palm wine, palm oil, and other such things for their daily sustenance.[182]

The ships that trade on the *Coast* are wily ones; there are those that sail half the time in *Caparie* [as privateers] and half the time in *Cofardie* [as merchants], and they have, at times, three or four types of scales with them by which the abovementioned black *Marckedors,* in their haste and when they do not pay careful attention, have often been cheated; which does not easily occur at the castles where there are usually true troy weights, both for the Blacks as well as for the Christians.[183]

Regarding the adulteration of gold, which occurs mostly from Samma to Breku and all the trading places between, it has now become quite common, so that at times the Blacks make two out of one *Lod* of good gold, [122] which has brought harm to many who do not know how to prove it;[184] indeed even to those who have been in the country continuously for ten or twelve years. For this adulteration they usually buy all kinds of coins which are not of pure silver, which are sold to them by the Christians, to their own corruption, thus assisting the one *Natureller* more than the other in the country in this and other similar activities, which in the end is to their [the Christians'] own injury;[185] of which much could be said but must be omitted for the sake of brevity. Therefore, this must be enough about the description of gold, whereupon I shall leave the *Gold Coast* and go on to the *Slave Coast,* of which I shall now give a brief description.

CHAPTER NINE

About the Slave Trade

On the ships which are intended for use in the slave trade [**123**] proper arrangements must be made, principally before they leave Europe, and this must be done in a far different way from that done for those which go to other *Coasts* for other types of trade.

1. With partitions so that male slaves and female slaves can be kept separated and apart from one another.[186]

2. Equipped with hand mills by which to grind their daily food, *Millie* or Turkish wheat, which is bought for that purpose in the country or has already been purchased by order at the fortresses before the ships have arrived.[187]

3. With as many more water barrels than usual as are calculated sufficient for each man on board, sailing from the *Coast* to the West Indies, to have two *Potter* of water daily for five or six months.[188]

4. With provisions based upon the extent of the journey, and [**124**] at any rate as much barley as possible, in the event *Millie* becomes expensive in the country because of war or other causes, which often happens.[189]

5. With provision of as many iron bolts as there will be slaves purchased, since each male slave alone, or at least two together, will always be kept in irons on board because near land they try to swim away, and, at times, have every intention of rising in rebellion aboard ship.[190]

6. That they must also carry enough wooden bowls and ship's kettles, according to *calculation* and reckoning, since these things are not available on the Coast.

7. [That] there is usually allotted for each slave on the journey ten *Potter* of Danish brandy that might be needed in the event of illness or for other possible

reasons; as well as straw mats and [125] simple blankets for each one, according to their number.[191]

8. The ship must also be provided with a chief barber and two assistants, as well as with good *medicines*, so that illness, such as dysentery, or other [ailments], should they occur among the slaves, can be treated in time or prevented.[192]

9. One must always have a fishing boat with the ship so that each man on board can get refreshment at those places where the ship anchors at rivers or in bays, as well as near land.

10. For the purchase of these slaves one must have arranged [to carry] the cargo [of wares] that are used there [i. e., on the Slave Coast]: *Bossies* or *Snoge-Pander*;[193] *Fufu* or very coarse Schleswig [Silesian] canvas; light iron rods; brass basins of a good one or one and one-half foot's width; pewter plates and pots of poor *manggods*; metal bracelets; large fish hooks; white beads or [126] glass beads; and other large, black *dito* [ditto] with white stripes on them, which are called *Conte Crebe*;[194] stoneware mugs with lids of poor *manggods*; and quantities of ordinary cloth of low value. This is the correct cargo for the [purchase of] slaves, indeed from the fortresses there are often given even other things, such as knives and such things, which are no longer in fashion at their place on the *Coast* and can, therefore, not be disposed of, since changes in the trade occur every year.[195]

11. One must always have on board a *Cabusee* or merchant from the fortresses who is knowledgeable about that trade, and give him a certain sum of money, agreed upon beforehand, or a little for each slave; who [i. e. the merchant] remains on board until one has the full consignment of slaves, after which, with a written report of all the circumstances, he returns [127] in his canoe, or boat, to his home which is at the foot of the fort. Otherwise, at times one takes aboard, from the

fortress, an assistant or an assistant merchant who has lived in the land for a long time and can speak the country's Portuguese, when it is necessary and no one else on the ship is experienced in this; he, in like manner, with permission from the ship, and with a written report, makes his way back to the fortress.[196]

The three true slave places, which lie east of the *Acara* kingdom and past the *River Volta*, are *Arder, Fida* [Whydah], and *Popo,* which trade in nothing but slaves, for the abovementioned wares, so that several thousand slaves are taken away annually by the English, French, and Dutch, all three of whom have their lodges there.[197] And though one often gets slaves on the *Gold Coast,* and in times of war even [128] more than one wants, yet it is not certain enough to depend on, which is why the true *Slave Coast* is always sought by everyone.[198] Indeed even at the ship's usual arrival at the *fortresses* [on the Gold Coast] after their having carried out arrangements and orders, and a number of slaves had been purchased [beforehand] and kept ready for the journey to be undertaken as quickly as possible, still one always goes to the slave places, where one lies at anchor in an open roadstead in good anchoring ground, indeed it is difficult to go ashore because of the aforementioned strong flow of the sea and current found there in the Bight.[199]

The land there, compared to the place before, is quite different in every way, in that it is very flat and fertile everywhere, with great quantities of grain, cattle, and other things. The inhabitants at that place are far more intelligent than the ones before, indeed they brew beer and bake bread as well as is done in Europe, and weave [129] a variety of pretty blankets of cotton worth 10, 20, and 30 *rixdalers.*[200] There are also found in the country some stones called *Agrii* and *Arder* beads which are valued on the *Gold Coast* as highly as gold, and, at times, even more highly. They appear to be a kind of blue jasper and there are some with other colors mixed in and are quite lovely to see.[201]

The aforementioned *Bossies,* or *Snoge-Pander,* which are a variety of small sea-snail shells and have originally come from East India where they are gathered on the shore, are used there in the same way that small coins are used in Europe, so that there is daily, among the inhabitants, purchase and sale for great amounts of money.[202]

These *Negroes* do not know much about the use of hand guns, but they all use large lances, hand arrows and a kind of large, curved pole, but no guns; for which reason the *Negroes* from *Acara,* all [130] of whom know very well how to handle guns, often make surprise attacks on them and cause great damage.[203]

It is remarkable to reflect on how these people can acquire all the slaves which are sold here every year, about which there are a number of opinions. Some say that they are acquired through their merchants many miles from there in exchange for their country's wares; others that they win them in war and battle; and still others that they steal and snatch away at the borders all they can lay their hands on, and that to this end they keep several thousand men, all year, everywhere on the roads and paths; however, all this does not give the true picture; but, according to their own report, all the kingdoms and provinces around there know that the true slave trade is in *Arder, Fida,* and *Popo,* so they go there daily with slaves for sale, from a good eighty miles inland, thus from day to day they always have [131] enough slaves. Yet it does happen there that when some ships are anchored at those places many a free *Negro* is stolen at night and carried aboard secretly; indeed fathers sell sons and sons fathers, so there is no conscience of any kind to be found there.[204]

Now I have run briefly through the entire *Coast* and reported, with the greatest simplicity, a little about all the types of trade which are carried on there; whereupon, as promised earlier, there shall now follow a little about various things in the entire land in general.

⚜ CHAPTER TEN ⚜

About religion, crops, animals, fish, reptiles

Throughout the entire country there are some *Negroes* who, in Portuguese are called *Fitisseiro,* and in the language of the country *Comfu* [i.e. ɔkɔmfoɔ, "spiritualist-healer"], who are clearly wizards so that with Satan's help they can predict the future, which later proves to be true, [**132**] although it does often prove wrong.[205]

These people are used by the *Natureller* for all manner of things, so that nothing of importance is undertaken or carried out before they give their consent, which however, does not happen before he [*Comfu*], upon payment from the petitioner, has made various sacrifices in the bush, at crossroads, and on the shore and other places, when he finally announces his opinion of what seems best for them to do or refrain from doing, which the *Natureller,* thereupon, must accept precisely as the proven and true faith. In the event that that advice proves to have a fortunate outcome, as predicted, be it in war or business, marriage, or anything else, it is considered to be the *Fetisseiro* alone, with his sacrificing and sanctity, [**133**] who has made it happen. If, however, the outcome is not as predicted, which often happen, and they complain about it to that *Fitisseiro,* and demand that he be brought to trial before the chief *Fitisseiros,* then he knows exactly how to excuse himself in every way, such as that the sacrifice was too poor, that the place where the sacrifice was made was unclean, or with other excuses, which the *Natureller* believe and dare not contradict; but they must often, on the contrary, provide another sacrifice which is better and finer, at their own greatest expense and to the profit of the *Fitissiero* who enjoys the best of it. Meanwhile, these poor people are forced into a number of things which they must unstintingly observe and follow, which are called *Fitissie,* such as that they must not wear in their clothing the colors red, white, or gray or any other color forbidden by him, or that they must not eat this or that kind of fruit, fish or meat, and more of such things.[206]

[134] Furthermore, that same *Fitisseiro* ordains for each person on which days he shall sacrifice and which days he shall keep holy, which among these people is Tuesday, just as ours is Sunday; and again, he tells them which days will be the best for work, so that their work will be successful and make good progress.[207]

There are also some among the wealthy and those who have sufficient resources who have a sacred object (in their opinion) in their houses, which is also called *Fitissie,* which has been made and given him by a *Fitisseiro,* after the latter had asked many questions about his birthday, his parents and father's *Fitissie,* and other similar questions; it is either a special image of clay or a stuffed bird or a snake skin or even a stone or some other such thing, which the *Fitisseiro* puts into a calabash [135] along with a number of small wild fruits, grass, bird feathers, and the other such things, so that it lies among them; to which *Fitissie* and sacred object each person shows great honor, keeping it near his head where he sleeps at night, and in everything he does he shows it respect and has confidence in it, as if all his fortune would depend on it. Indeed when he has a suspicion that one of his slaves has committed one or another form of roguery the slave must swear on it; and there is very much more which is too extensive to be described. All this aforementioned madness is accepted, observed, and believed unstintingly and absolutely by each of them, without anyone daring to transgress the least of what he has been ordered to do by the *Fitisseiro,* and this is largely because the *Fitisseiros* apparently can perform a number of tricks (much like conjuring) and other witchcraft with [136] snakes, lions, tigers, and other animals, with Satan's help. Many such acts have been described, and I, myself, have seen a great number which would be considered unbelievable.[208]

Finally there is this to note, that all the inhabitants in the Kingdom of *Acara* (apart from the Qvambus) have their children circumcised when they are more than seven years old, like the Jews; which, however, is not done anywhere else on the entire *Coast.*[209] But in all other things, their belief in the *Fetisseiros'* magic in everything is found throughout the land.

Fruits and grain which are found in the land:

1. *Millie, Agio,* or Turkish wheat is planted by the *Natureller* before the *travat* season, as are peas in Europe, which are the foods most consumed on the entire Coast, both for daily food [137] as well as for sale, frequently, for other wares, since a single seed produces several hundred.[210]

2. *Small Millie, Agiu Cacraba,* grows in every way like flat tubes in the marshes in this country; it is sown in the same way as hemp and is of the same size, of which a single seed produces more than a thousand; and it is nearly as good as rye and very useful for the inhabitants.[211]

3. and 4. *Aduba* are two kinds of beans, the one quite gray, like Turkish beans, the other quite red, like large sugar peas; they are sown and harvested like the European varieties.[212]

5. *Acrossa,* or *Ataqvea,* is a fruit as large as a hazel nut, and is planted like the beans. But it multiplies underground in great numbers without growing up above ground, where no more of it is seen than a little grass, and it tastes like almonds. [138]

6. *Mallagette, Ewissia, Greyn* or *Paradiskorn* is a kind of false pepper, sown like buckwheat and grows to resemble it.

7. *Pegla,* or rice, is acquired mostly on the *Boven Coast* (which is from *Rio Sierra Liona* to the *Gold Coast*) is in every way like our oats in appearance, both when it is growing and later when it ripens [213]

The abovementioned varieties are not sown more than once a year, which is at the end of March and beginning of April, and are harvested in June and July, which is from and after *travat* season [*sic*].[214]

Following are the fruits which are grown throughout the year:

8. *Brambas,* or small citrons grow wild and in great quantities throughout the country.[215]

9. *Oranie* apples, or bitter oranges, grow in the same way as the small citrons.[216] [139]

10. *Aguiree* is sugar cane, which the Portuguese know very well how to make into sugar; but the inhabitants in the country use it for nothing other than daily consumption.[217]

11. *Patattas* are in every way like our Jerusalem, or earth, artichokes; they are planted annually and are very pleasant to eat.[218]

12. *Enyamos* is a kind of root, very large and in appearance absolutely like a long, homemade loaf, of which one root weighs twenty-eight pounds, and it is planted annually.[219]

13. *Bannanas,* or *Broddi,* is a fruit which is unlike anything in Europe, grows wild everywhere, and is very pleasant both in appearance and in taste.

14. *Baccoves* grow in the same way as the former but are smaller and much more delicious in aroma and taste.[220]

15. *Annassa* is a fruit whose virtues cannot be adequately described; considered [140] to be the best fruit in the world, it grows with a crown on top like an artichoke, and resembles a pomegranate but is much larger. It grows wild everywhere.[221]

16, 17, 18. *Arisseba, Afoteba,* and *Asnamba* are two [sic] varieties of plums which grow wild everywhere on the Coast.[222]

19. *Turreba* resembles a large apple in every way, [its] inside full of small seeds like a cucumber, it grows wild everywhere on the ground on some thistles [? thistle-like plants].[223]

20. *Pigomento, Apperaba,* or Spanish pepper is like a long raisin in appearance, grows wild everywhere in the country on small brush, and is very much like mustard.[224]

21. *Colla* is a fruit which is like a large chestnut, grown in a shell or pod like large Welsh beans, is used very much by the Natives, eaten raw, when they are drinking.[225]

22. *Poponer, Papay,* or *Spansk Spek* grows on tall trees, mostly [141] on the *Boven Coast,* it grows wild and resembles a gourd.[226]

23. *Cocos-Nødder* also grow wild on large, tall trees that look like palms, but they grow mostly on the *Boven Coast.*[227]

These then are all of the earth's fruits in the entire land, apart from the palm tree from which they get their palm wine daily, and, from small red nuts which grow on them, they get that wonderful palm oil which is used both in place of butter and for healing. With the branches they thatch their houses, and of the fibers they make their fishing equipment and other things.[228]

The domestic cattle and animals are these:

Cows and bulls, sheep, goats, pigs, chickens, and a few horses which come from *Arder* and the *Slave Coast,* which is the only place they are found. The cows and bulls are much smaller than the European ones, and the cows are not milked, nor is any butter churned.[229] [142] There are no tame geese, ducks, or turkey hens, and even though they are often brought there by the Christians, they usually die straightaway.[230]

The wild animals are:[231]

Elephants, lions, buffaloes, elands, hart, three varieties of roe deer, *Steen Bukke,* tiger, leopards, wolves, civet cats, large porcupines, hares, four other varieties of forest cat, namely *Cuocubu, Adompo, Agviri,* and *Abakaw,* and five varieties of small and large apes; which animals are all well-known to the inhabitants who destroy as many as possible.[232]

The Wild birds are:

Four varieties of wild hens, four varieties of wild pigeon, ducks, geese, four varieties of snipe, large eagles, falcons, hawks, herons, blue parrots, crows, and other innumerable quantities of small and large unknown birds in large flocks. The Christians at all the forts raise many tame pigeons, but **[143]** this is not done anywhere among the *Natureller*.[233]

Fish which are caught along the *Coast* mostly before and after the *travat* season:[234]

> 1. *Abuje* is a variety of ruff, no larger than roach, which is always caught on the *Coast* and tastes good.[235]

> 2. *Wiwrye* is as large as a tench [or doctor fish] and nearly of the same appearance, except that it is covered with scales.[236]

> 3. *Ebbang*, called *Sarding* by the Portuguese; is in every way like our small herring and is caught in great numbers.[237]

> 4. *Saqviri* is like a small herring apart from the head which resembles a hawk's beak, from which there are two long fins reaching to the end of the fish, by which it flies up out of the water and moves for a distance of a good *cannon* shot before it again falls into the water, so it is called "flying fish".[238]

> 5, *Saffro* resembles a mackerel, except that it is much larger and its tail is shaped like a half-moon.[239] **[144]**

> 6, *Suqvi* is like a small trout, but without spots, and it has a growth of gristle on its mouth, so it is called "snub-nose."[240]

> 7. *Tantara* resembles our ray with one exception, that [is,] its tail is a little shorter and it has no sharp spike at the end.[241]

8. *Dorado* is a very delicious fish and lovely to see, especially in the water where it appears to shine like gold, with flecks all over the body, like salmon or trout, of which the largest are four and one-half feet long.[242]

9. *Ekara Samman* is like a *kolle* with scales covering the entire body, but the meat is so full of small bones that it can be eaten only out of necessity, therefore it is called *Pisse Diable,* or "devil's fish."[243]

10. *Esua* is a shark and is called *Tubaron* by the Portuguese, the largest being about 9 feet long; it is often caught on the *Coast* and eaten by the *Natureller,* but not by the Christians since with great greed it eats dead people who [145] have been thrown overboard, as well as all other carrion.[244]

11. *Equiri*, called *See-Snoek* by the Dutch, is in taste and in every other way like our pike but much larger and longer.[245]

12. *Ewa,* or *Corcobado,* is almost as wide as it is long, in size like a bream and caught daily by the Natives, mostly among the rocks, but does not taste good.[246]

13. *Etiri* is a variety of very large ray, called "sea devil" by the Christians, has a very sharp tail completely covered with sharp spines, and is very ferocious in appearance; it is not eaten by the Christians and the *Natureiler* hardly dare catch it.[247]

14. *Tarsere* is a variety of sea bream, called *Pargos* by the Portuguese, the fish which is caught in the greatest quantities in the kingdom of *Acara*, as described earlier.[248]

15. *Albo Cora* is a large, broad fish, five or six feet long, very [146] dry in flavor and without scales, has a tail like a half-moon and is caught in large quantities in the Spanish Sea and in the area before the *Guinea Coast* begins.[249]

16. and 17. *Coreth* and *Bonith* appear, beyond a doubt,

to be of the same variety as *Albo Cora*, since they are the same in all respects, but much smaller.[250]

18. *Pussedansas* are lobsters, like the *European* variety, except that the claws are not nearly as large.[251]

19. *Allantees,* or oysters, are much larger than those caught in *Europe;* there are also some small ones which grow in the trees growing near the rivers.[252]

20. *Appafiahis,* or mussels, are like the European variety.[253]

21. *Krintria,* or crabs, like those in *Europe,* are found both in the sea and on land.

22. *Harders* are a variety of lagoon fish and are like small lavaret.[254]

23. *Batavia,* or small carp, [147] are, like the previous type, fresh lagoon fish.[255]

These are the names of many of the fish caught along the entire *Coast,* where they are fished mostly with hooks on lines of bast, small harpoons with a fluke and, in the lagoons, with nets.[256] At times the *Natureller* catch strange and unknown fish which are very remarkable in appearance and whose names are not known, and they are not eaten but are considered a sort of sea wonder or prophecy of some kind of change to come.[257]

Reptiles and other such creatures:

1. Five varieties of snakes are found, of which the largest, called *Owua,* is so large that the skin taken from one is four and one-half feet wide, and others are like those in the countries here.[258]

2. *Leguaner* are a variety of large lizard, eaten by the Christians, and living near the rivers in the country.[259] [148]

3. *Aggedisser* are true lizards and are seen everywhere daily, they do no harm and are not hated by anyone, so that they go around nearly tame everywhere.[260]

4. There are two varieties of *Scorpioner;* the one as small as shrimp, which are often found among books and papers, four or five together, for which one feels no fear of their poison since certain remedies are known. The other variety are as large as full-size crabs, very dangerous, and their poison is almost impossible to be rid of.[261]

5. The *Tusind-Been,* or *Onye,* is like a large cabbage worm and appears to have a thousand legs; it is found mostly at night, when it comes and stings and injures people, and the sore is almost incurable.[262]

6. *Kaymanos* are a variety of *crocodile* which are found in the rivers and are often caught, of which the largest are seven feet long.

7. The really large *crocodiles* are found, for the most part, in *Rio Gambia* and *Rio* **[149]** *de Volta,* but usually not anywhere else.[263]

These are the reptiles and insects [*sic*] which are most known here, although there are found countless other types, both large and small, whose names are not known since they are not seen as often as the above named.

CHAPTER ELEVEN

Now follow the wares which are carried from Europe to Guinea and traded there[264]

1. Stamped iron bars.[265]

2. Copper rods.[266]

3. Large and small brass cauldrons with a thick iron ring around the middle.[267]

4. Brass basins of from one to four foot *Vielse.*[268]

5. Metal bracelets.[269]

6. Pewter plates, bowls, canisters, and other things of poor *Manggods.*[270]

7. Padlocks of five varieties [? sizes].[271]

8. Three varieties of knives with sheaths.[272]

9. Fish hooks of three varieties.[273]

10. Jew's harps.[274] **[150]**

11. Large pins and sewing needles.

12. Small files.

13. Light Utrecht guns comprising *fusils, carbines, muskets*, and low quality pistols, all with flintlocks and not any with matchlocks.[275]

14. Coarse *Slange-krud* in small barrels of up to 10, 25, and 50 pounds.[276]

15. Hewn flintstones.

16. Earthenware mugs with lids and without lids.[277]

17. *Fyrstaal.*[278]

18. *Bossies* or "snake skulls."[279]

19. Nine varieties of large and small glass beads in all colors.[280]

20. Blood coral of the largest size.[281]

21. Ordinary mirrors of a quarter [sic] in height.[282]

22. Tobacco pipes.

23. Ordinary black and other tobacco.[283]

24. Tallow in small barrels of 10 pounds.[284]

25. *Flaske-fodere* filled with grain and French brandies.[285]

26. Brandy in ankers.[286]

27. Old sheeting, washed and well-packed in chests.[287] **[151]**

28. Ordinary *Slesisk* [Silesian] canvas in small pieces [lengths].[288]

29. Coarse *dito* [ditto] in large pieces, called *Fufu*.[289]

30. East Indian cottons, namely *Zitsen, Taffezeles,* blue *Baftas, Necanesser, Tapetanteinos, Salampuris, Pentades,* table cloths, dust cloths, and other whole pieces of multi-colored cottons.[290]

31. Striped canvas cloth.

32. English, Dutch, and Bremen *Say*.[291]

33. *Perpetuaner,* of which the English is the best.[292]

34. Striped Turkish *Grosgrøn*.[293]

35. Cheap red cloth.

36. All sorts of linen and woolen cloths made in *Europe,* the more colorful the better.

37. Red, yellow, and blue silk ribbons costing four or five shillings an *alen* in *Europe*.[294]

38. Old, reblocked hats with sham bands on them.[295] **[152]**

Regarding other things such as small brass chains, red ac, wooden and tin buckets, and similar small things, they are not much in demand because the ordinary man on the ships and on land barters them for fruits, parrots, monkeys, and other similar things.[296]

For those wares the following are received in Guinea:[297]

1. Gold.[298]

2. *Ambergris,* which is obtained most at the *River Gambia.*[299]

3. *Civet.*[300]

4. Elephant and sea cow tusks.[301]

5. Wax.

6. Rice.[302]

7. *Greyn* or Paradise corn.[303]

8. Hides of buffalo, eland, hart, and Bukke.[304]

9. Red wood.[305]

10. Mats of reeds and straw.[306]

11. Salt from the kingdom of *Acara,* but not much. [**153**]

12. Sugar from the island *St. Thomé,* and preserved sweets, all of which wares are taken back to *Europe.*[307]

13. The *Agrii* or *Arder beads* which are bought in the *Bight* are sold again with great profit on the *Gold Coast.*[308]

14. Cotton cloth which is bought on the *Boven Coast* and in the *Bight* is traded in the same way on the *Gold Coast,* with profit.[309]

15. Slaves, which are taken all the way to West India.

As regards snail shells, mussel shells, monkeys, parrots, and all such small articles which are not considered to be of any value, they are traded, as described above, for other cheap articles.[310]

63

CHAPTER TWELVE
Conclusion

I shall now recall a few items which are useful and necessary for the sailor and trader to know.

1. Before one sails to this *Guinea Coast,* one must pay careful attention to the fact that the [154] worst time of year to sail among the islands which are called the "salted islands" (which lie west-northwest of *Cabo Verde* and are called the *Hesperides* in Latin) and that *Coast* are in the months of *September* and *October,* since at that time there is very often calm there, and changeable winds; where many a ship has had to lie and idle for a long time, and thus suffer great harm. Such was the experience of three Danish ships, the new *Kiøbenhavns Vaaben, Gyldenlewes Vaaben,* and the galliot *Luavervigen,* in the year 1690 in those months,[311] in that for several weeks they lay becalmed between those islands and the *Guinea Coast,* during which time a number of their people were burdened by extreme illness, with the result that twenty-two persons died. And when, at the end of November, they finally sailed into *Rio Sierra Liona,* most of their people, [of] both high and low [status] were badly tormented by rickets and other illnesses, [155] so that some of these died at the river and some on land. For this reason every single person should take good care of himself.[312]

2. Although there is, for the most part, at every trading place along the *Coast,* very good anchoring ground, yet at *Acara* this is not found to be the case, where there is foul ground everywhere, so the anchor must be weighed every day, or at least every other day, if one does not want to lose it, to which many a one can bear witness by his damages.[313]

3. One must be particularly careful in the *travat,* or rainy seasons, which are in the months of April, May, and

June, not to anchor, from *Sierra Liona* to *Tessie*, closer to land than one mile, because at those times there come just as strong *travats*, or rain clouds, from sea as from land; therefore one must see to it that, [156] before this happens, one enters a river or bay in good weather, where one can remain safe from all danger.[314]

4. The inhabitants are not willing to come out to the ships to trade during the rainy season, just as they are unwilling in the month of February, since in that month the air is very cold and, for them, unhealthful, along the entire Coast, which [season] they call *Armetanen*, but is called *Canarii* by the English.[315] Therefore the best times of the year to trade everywhere on the Coast are the months of January, March, July, August, September, October, November, and December, [a fact] by which every Guinea traveler is usually guided.[316]

5. When anyone from the kingdom of *Acara* (which is reckoned to lie 1417 miles[317] from the city of royal residence, Copenhagen) or from the last trading places on the *Gold Coast, Tessie* and *Nungo,* intends to make his way home to the Fatherland again, or to go back to [157] *Qvaqva, Tusk,* or *Greyn Coasts,* to trade there, he must not even consider sailing back along the Coast from which he has come earlier, since this can only be done with the greatest trouble and difficulty, because he must sail with the sea breeze every sixth hour and then again, every sixth hour, he must anchor under the land breeze; for this reason everyone who wishes to go back there sails right from the coast to the Line [Equator], as far up as he can, which is a better way to make progress on the journey because of the strong current which runs within the *Bight*.[318] Once one has come so high on this course that the three islands *Ile de Prince, de St. Thomé,* and *d'Annobou,* all of which belong to the Portuguese, are leeward of the ship, one usually puts in there because of what one can get there;[319] namely, on *Ile de Prince* and *d'Annabou,* rice, chickens, pigs,

coconuts, pawpaws, [158] and other excellent fruits, as well as water; yet all these things are available in much greater quantities on *Ile de St. Thomé*, and even, at times, a great amount of sugar in addition.³²⁰ Indeed there are also found on these islands some wild *Steen-Bukke*, very much like the European roe deer, which are often shot for provisions, and this is done best when one has dogs on the ships because none are found on land; nor could they live there long because of the great heat.³²¹

On this island *St. Thomé*, which lies just under the Line and right between the other two, there is a castle with a Portuguese *garrison* which is well equipped, where many Christians of the *Catholic* faith live, who cultivate the land with their slaves.³²² But on the other two there are no forts since they are under the command of the *Governor* on *St. Thomé*; and on each of them there lives only [159] a single Christian person with a number of Blacks.³²³

6. At these islands, just as at all the rivers, *Gabon, Sierra Liona,* and others, one must trust no ship, be it small or large, unless one is well acquainted with it and is secured in every way against it, if one wants to be out of danger.³²⁴

7. One has a very good opportunity in the *River Gabon,* which lies a little east of *Cabo de Lopo Consalves* [Cape Lopez], to clean the ships and to take on wood and other wares, but not water; this is done at a small island in the same river, an island called *Prince-Eylandt* but called *Papagoje Eylandt* [Parrot Island] by most people, where, on the western shore of the river there live Blacks who own the island, and their highest chief, whom they call the *Prince,* who usually stay there with the Christians as long as the latter are there, for which reason they always have their huts standing on the island.³²⁵ But as soon [160] as the ships have sailed off again, they row [*sic*] their small canoes or fishing boats back to the mainland. And they themselves carry aboard the wares which are found on that same western shore, which

are: elephant tusks, sea cow [hippopotamus] tusks, wax, monkeys, parrots, mats, and all kinds of fruit, for which they are given the same wares as in *Rio Sierra Liona*.[326]

They showed great honor to their Prince, who in the year 1692 was a very old Black, by immediately holding a cloth in front of his eyes when he drank, and the entire assembly of Blacks covered their faces at the same time, so that no one would see it.[327]

8. On the eastern shore of the same river, two good miles mostly east-southeast from the abovementioned island, there lives a king whose power over the people is far greater than [that of] the afore-mentioned Prince, yet with whom he often wages war, since the river farther upstream [161] is sometimes dry, so they can approach one another.[328] If one wants to trade in that king's city [*sic*] where all the Blacks who live on the eastern shore usually assemble, one may, without any fear or danger, sail right up to the place with the boat and wares, and one can then stay there as long as one likes; the city lies a half mile north-northeast of the river, on a hill, and is a *cannon* shot in length, where the king lives who, in the year 1692 was a very young Black.

9. Finally there is this reminder, as mentioned briefly earlier, that it is very advantageous to carry a fishing boat on all the ships, by which means one can catch as much fish as one wants everywhere along the entire *Coast,* and thus not only can one always get provisions but also save a great deal on the diet for the journey home; the English have been very industrious in this respect, in that [162] hardly a single one of their ships comes to the *Coast* without having been provided with a boat, besides which they have one at all their *fortresses* and *lodges,* by which all the garrisons support themselves to a great extent; and with little trouble, and without any expense, they acquire, daily, a great quantity for their food and subsistence.

This, then, is briefly that which I have observed by experience and careful research and have considered necessary to report about the country Guinea, to which I have made two journeys, and where I have stayed for nine years, during which time I have traveled everywhere in the rivers and on land.[329] That I now allow it to be printed is purely that I seek to serve my Fatherland and particularly those out there who sail to that country [**163**] to trade, so I trust that it will be looked upon kindly by the gentle readers, and not be totally rejected because it is nothing more than a simple account by an uneducated pen and not presented in an elevated historical style and with great eloquence (which would have been beyond my capabilities). And just as I can at least assure them that all things are truly found to be as they have been presented here in all simplicity, so do I hope that it will be accepted, at least until such time as something better and more detailed appears.

End of Erick Tilleman's text

COPENHAGEN

Printed by Hans Pedersen in the year 1697.

CHRONOLOGY OF THE THREE CASTLES

Elmina [*St. George d'el Mina*]

1482 built by Portuguese

1637 conquered by Dutch

1637-1872 Dutch conquered headquarters on Gold Coast

1872 becomes British possession by treaty

Cape Coast [originally *Carolusburg*]

1653 built for Swedes by Carlof

1658 take-over by Carlof for Denmark

1659 (April 15-16) given to Dutch by Smidt

1659 (May) Fetu take-over

1660 Fetu sell it to Swedes

1660-1662 in Swedish hands

1663 Fetu take-over again, sell to Dutch

1664 British take-over under Capt. Robert Holmes

1664-1876 British headquarters on Gold Coast

Christiansborg

1653 lodge at Osu built by Swedes

1658 Danes take over

1659 Dutch take over

1661 Jost Cramer acquires land for Denmark-Norway and builds fort

1679 sold to Portuguese

1679-1683 in Portuguese hands as Fort S. Francisco Xavier

1683 Portuguese return it to Danes

1693 Akwamu seize Castle

1694 Danes recover Castle by purchase

1694-1850 Danish headquarters on Gold Coast

1850 sold to British

1877 British colonial government moved to Accra and Christiansborg Castle made seat of government

1957–present seat of government of the Republic of Ghana

GLOSSARY

adels-burser a soldier who performs the duties of a corporal or patrol leader. The term is still used today in the Netherlands signifying a rank higher than a private but lower than an officer.

agrii beads aggrey beads usually blue; a highly valued bead purchased in Popo or Benin and sold on the Gold Coast.

alen a linear measure, 1 alen = 68. 81 cm.

anker 38-39 liters.

baftas a coarse, cheap cotton cloth from India, usually blue.

banco weight slightly heavier than troy weight, 9:8.

bomba an African supervisor or overseer. The term was not used in gold mining operations alone, but was general for the position. See Isert (1992) 189, 195.

Boven Coast from Dutch, Upper Coast, referring to the stretch of Guinea coast starting at Sierra Leone and extending to the Gold Coast, where it gives way to the Lower Coast.

bossies from Portuguese *búzio,* cowrie shells.

brafu Akan *bráfó*, the official executioner. An important officer in the Akan governmental system.

cabusee from Portuguese *caboceiro*, chief or headman. The term, in a number of variations, was used generally by all the early European sources.

caparie piracy.

cannon shot approximately 1 kilometer. See Nörregaard (1966) 23.

cofardie merchant shipping.

comfu Akan ɔkɔmfoɔ ("spiritualist-healer"), interpreter of the category of spiritual agents known as *abosom* (sg., ɔbosom). See Christaller (1933).

Commaté Tilleman's term for the deity worshipped from Cape

Verde to Cape Tagrin. I have not found this term in other sources. Perhaps it is a Tilleman's own combination of terms he met later on the Gold Coast: Akan *Onyàmé* and Fante *Onyankome* ("Supreme Being, God"). See also Jones (1985) 176 n. 156.

conte crebe a black bead with white stripes. See Jones (1985) 313.

dambas Akan *dàmmas*, a small quantity of gold weighed by using the red seed of the *plant* Abrus precatorius.

double land/double forest commonly used terms to indicate that one stretch of land/forest is visible at the shore and another one behind the seaboard.

equipage-mester the officer in charge of stores, particularly of the dock house.

fendrich officer of low rank. The term is non-translatable.

fiscal treasurer.

Fitissie/Fitisseiro from Portuguese *feitiço*, magic or artificial. The term was used universally, and condescendingly, as a rule, by the Europeans to describe religious practices and practitioners.

fjerding a quarter of a land mile 1.9 kilometers.

flaske-fødere cases especially constructed for the transport of bottles.

forlaeser lay reader or cantor

fufu Akan term for white, here specifically to signify white cloth.

fusil a light flintlock firearm.

fyrstaal steel used with flint to produce a spark.

gefriedere synonymous to adels-burser (above).

grosgrøn grogram. Loosely woven fabric of silk and wool, often stiffened with gum.

interloper a ship operating independently of any company or nation. See Jones (1985) 315.

kakara Akan *kakrá*, little, small, few. Used in the gold trade to indicate gold of little value.

lerret? canvas, a tightly woven cotton cloth

lod 1 lod = 15. 625 trade weight until 1861.

Lybsk seebier beer from Lübeck.

magasin-mester officer in charge of stores

manggods a low quality alloy of tin and lead, pewter

marckedor from Portugese *mercador*, merchant.

mil 1 land mile – 7. 5 kilometers/ 1 sea mile = 7. 4 kilometers. Presumably Tilleman referred to sea miles when giving sailing distance between places on the coast, and land miles when indicating locations on land.

momme a strong, dark beer originally brewed in Brunschweig.

Natureller native Africans. The term was not in general use in the written sources.

necanesser blue and white striped East Indian cotton, designated as "broad" and "narrow."

negeri a term generally used in Scandinavian sources to indicate African settlements, without any indication of size.

pargos? sea bream.

particuliere ships see interlopers.

pegla rice. Since Tilleman uses the term when describing the Sierra Leone area this is probably a misinterpretation of one of several possible terms from local languages: Temne *a-pδla*; Sherbro *pɛlɛ*, Limba *pakalaba*, Tonko Limba *paga*, Adam Jones (personal communication).

pentades probably *pintado*, printed East Indian cotton.

perpetuaner a high quality woolen cloth. See Jones (1985) 317.

pott/potter 1 pott = 9.68 liters/ 2 potter = 1 kanne.

profos in the sixteenth and seventeenth centuries a high-ranking officer in the infantry who was responsible for discipline and punishment.

rask rash, a smooth fabric made of silk or worsted.

rixdaler in the 1690s 256 rixdalers bought 1 pound of gold. Thus 1 rixdaler = .06 ounces of gold. See Meyer (1698) 1, 6.

say a finely woven woolen cloth resembling serge.

sek a white wine from southern Europe.

snoge-pander lit. snake skulls. The term was used generally in Scandinavia to indicate cowry shells, widely used to decorate bridles.

steen-bukke lit. a mountain goat/ram. Tilleman apparently used it, incorrectly, to identify a small antelope, possibly a duiker.

taffezelas taffeta. A glossy, woven textile.

taku beans Akan *tàkú,* a seed used to weigh small amounts of gold dust, a weight slightly heavier than the *damma*. (See above).

tapenteinos either *tappesendis,* an East Indian cotton printed on both sides, or *tapsel,* a blue and multi-colored striped cotton. See Heiden (1904) 555.

travat from Portuguese *trovoada* thunder storm. The term was widely used to indicate a line squall, common in the rainy season.

troy weight first used in Troyes, France for weighing gold, silver and precious stones. In this system the pound, divided into 12 ounces, weighs. 373 kilograms.

zitsen? chintz, an East Indian cotton, printed calico.

BIBLIOGRAPHY

Abbreviations

BIFAN *Bulletin de l'Institut Français/fondamental d'Afrique Noire*

CUP Cambridge University Press

CWAS Centre of West African Studies, Birmingham

HA *History in Africa*

JAH *Journal of African History*

OUP Oxford University Press

RA Rigsarkivet, Copenhagen

V-gK Vestindisk-guinea Kompaniet

Following the Scandinavian alphabets the three letters Æ, Ø/Ö/OE,Å, AA will appear at the end, in that order.

Abbiw, Daniel, K. *Useful Plants of Ghana* London, 1990.

Africa Pilot, vol. I, 12th edition, London, 1967.

Ajayi, J.F.A. and Crowder, Michael, eds. *History of West Africa* 2 vols.: London, 1977-78.

Alpern, Stanley B. "The European Introduction of Crops into West Africa in Precolonial Times," *HA* 19 (1992): 13-43.

Atlantic Ocean Pilot, London, 1884.

Baesjou, René. "The Historical Evidence in Old Maps and Charts of Africa with Special Referance to West Africa." *HA* 15 (1988): 1-83.

Barbot, Jean. *Barbot on Guinea: The writings of Jean Barbot on West Africa, 1678-1712*, 2 volumes, ed. P.E.H.Hair, Adam Jones, and Robin Law. London, 1992.

Bean, Richard. "A Note on the Relative Importance of Slaves and Gold in West African exports." *JAH* (1974): 351-56.

Blake, John W. *Europeans in West Africa 1450-1560*. 2 vols.: London, 1941-42.

—. *West Africa: Quest for God and Gold, 1454-1578*. London, 1977.

Blussé, Leonard and Femme Gaastra, eds. *Companies and Trade*. Leiden, 1981.

Boateng, E.A. *A Geography of Ghana*. Cambridge, 1970.

Bosman, William. *A New and Accurate Description of the Coast of Guinea*, London 1705, reprint with notes by J.D. Fage and R E. Bradbury. London, 1967.

Bredsdorff, Asta. "Fregatten *Charlotta Amalia*'s Mærkelige Skaebne." *Arbog 1975 af Selskabet Handels – og søfartsmuseets Venner*, 22-41.

Brenner, Louis. "'Religious' Discourses in and About Africa" in *Discourse and its Disguises: The Interpretation of African Oral Texts*, ed. Karin Barber and P.F. de Moraes Farias. Birmingham, 1989, 87-103.

Christaller, J.G. *Dictionary of the Asante and Fante Language Called Tshi*. 2d. edition, Basel, 1933.

Claridge, W. Walton. *A History of the Gold Coast and Ashanti*. 2 vols.: London, 1964.

Daaku, Kwame Y. *Trade and Politics on the Gold Coast, 1600-1720*. Oxford, 1970.

Dampier, William. *A New Voyage Round the World*. London 1697.

Dapper, Olfert. *Umbestandliche und eigentliche Beschriebung von Africa*. Amsterdam, 1670.

Davies, K.G. *The Royal African Company*. London, 1957.

DeCorse, Christopher R. "Culture Contact, Continuity, and Change on the Gold Coast, AD 1400-900." *African Archaeological Review* 10 (1992): 163-96.

—. "West African Archaeology and the Atlantic Slave Trade." *Slavery and Abolition* 12 (1991): 92-96.

—. "Beads as Chronological Indicators in West African Archaeology: A Re-examination." *Beads Journal of the Society of Bead Researchers* 1 (1989): 41-53.

De Marees, Pieter. *Description and Historical Account of the Gold Kingdom of Guinea* (1602) trans. and ed, Albert Van Dantzig and Adam Jones. London, 1987.

Dickson, Kwamina B. *A Historical Geography of Ghana*. Cambridge, 1969.

Donnan, Elizabeth. *Documents Illustrative of the History of the Slave Trade to America*. 4 vols.: Washington, 1930.

Ehrencron-Müller, H. *Forfatterlexikon omfattende Danmark, Norge og Island indtil 1814*. Bind VIII, Copenhagen, 1930.

Erikson, Joan Mowat. *The Universal Bead*. New York, 1969.

Fage, John D. *A History of West Africa*. Cambridge, 1969.

—. "Some Remarks on Beads and trade in Lower Guinea in the Sixteenth and Seventeenth Centuries." *JAH* 3 (1962): 343-47.

—."More about Aggrey and Akori Beads" in *2000 Ans d'Histoire Africaine*. Paris, 1981, 205-211.

Feldbæk, Ole. "The Organization and Structure of the Danish East India, West India and Guinea Companies in the Seventeenth and Eighteenth Centuries" in *Companies and Trade*, ed. Leonard Blussé and Femme Gaastra, Leiden, 1981, 135-58.

Field, M.J. *Religion and Medicine of the Gã People*. Oxford, 1961.

Garrard, Timothy F. *Akan Weights and the Gold Trade*. London, 1980.

Gordon, Albert and Kahan, Leonard. *The Tribal Bead: A Hand-*

book of African Trade Beads. New York, 1976.

Grove, G.L. *Personalhistorisk Tidsskrift,* Femte Række, Bind I. Copenhagen, 1904.

Grove, Jean M. and A.M. Johansen. "The Historical Geography of the Volta Delta, Ghana, During the Period of Danish Influence." *BIFAN* 30B (1968): 1376-1421.

Hair, P.E.H. *The Atlantic Slave Trade and Black Africa.* Liverpool, 1989.

Heawood, Edward. *A History of Geographical Discovery in the Seventeenth and Eighteenth Centuries.* New York, 1965.

Heiden, Max. *Handworterbuch der Textil.* Stuttgart, 1904.

Henige, David. "John Kabes of Komenda: An Early African Entrepreneur and State Builder." *JAH* 18 (1977): 1-19.

Herskovits, Melville J. *Dahomey.* 2 vols.: New York, 1938.

Huber, Hugo. *The Krobo: Traditional Social and Religious Life of a West African People.* Bonn, 1963.

Isert, Paul Erdmann. *Journey to Guinea and the Caribbean Islands in Columbia (1788).* trans. and ed. Selena A. Winsnes, as *Letters on West Africa and the Slave Trade.* London, 1992.

Johnson, Marion. "The Cowrie Currencies of West Africa." *JAH* 11 (1970): 17-49, 331-53.

Jones, Adam. *German Sources for West African History, 1599-1669.* Wiesbaden, 1983.

—. *Brandenburg Sources for West African History.* Stuttgart, 1985.

Justesen, Ole. "Kolonierne i Africa" in *Kolonierne i Asien og Afrika,* ed. Ole Feldbæk and Ole Justesen. Copenhagen, 1980, 289-461.

Kalkar, Otto. *Ordbog til del Ældre Danske Sprog (1300-1700).* 5 vols.: Copenhagen, 1881-1918.

Kalous, Milan. "Akorite?" *JAH* 20 (1979): 203-17.

Kea, Ray A. *Settlements, Trade, and Politics in the Seventeenth Century Gold Coast.* Baltimore, 1982.

—. "Firearms and Warfare on the Gold and Slave Coasts From the Sixteenth to the Nineteenth Centuries." *JAH* 20 (1971): 185-213.

Kilson, Marion. *African Urban Kinsman: The Gã of Central Accra.* New York, 1974.

Kwamena-Poh, M.A. *Government and Politics in the Akuapem State, 1730-1850.* Evanston, 1976.

Kyerematen, A.A.Y. *Panoply of Ghana.* New York, 1964.

Labarthe, P. *Voyage à la Côte de Guinée ou Description des Côtes d'Afrique depuis le cap Tagrin jusqu' au cap de Lopez-Gonzalves.* Paris, 1805.

Labat, Jean-Baptiste. *Voyage du Chevalier des Marchais en Guinée, isles voisines et àt Cayenne.* Paris, 1730.

Law, Robin. "Between the Sea and the Lagoons: The Interaction of Maritime and Inland Navigation on the Precolonial Slave Coast." *Cahiers d études africaines* 29 (1989): 209-37.

—. *Correspondence from the Royal African Company and Factories at Offra and Whydah on the Slave Coast of West Africa in the Public Record Office, London 1678-93.* Edinburgh, 1990.

—. *The Slave Coast of West Africa, 1550-1750.* Oxford, 1991.

—. *Further Correspondence of the Royal African Company... , 1681-1699.* Madison, 1992.

Lawrence, A.W. *Trade Castles and Forts of West Africa.* London, 1963.

Little, K.L. *The Mende of Sierra Leone.* London, 1951.

Makepeace, Margaret. "English Traders on the Guinea Coast, 1657-1668: An Analysis of the East India Copany Archive." *HA* 16 (1989): 237-84.

Meyer, Hartvig. "History of Christiansborg," manuscript, Rigsarkivet, Copenhagen, Vestindisk – guinea Kompaniet, 187, 1 (698?), 7 folios.

Molbech, Christian. *Dansk Ordbog*. 2 vols.: Copenhagen, 1859.

Monrad, H.C. *Bidrag til en Skildring af Guinea-Kysten og dens Indbyggere*. Copenhagen, 1822.

Moore, David D. "Henrietta Marie. An Introduction to the First Slaver Studied in the New World." *Seafarer's Journal of Maritime Heritage* 1 (1987): 199-205.

Multilingual Glossary of Textile Terminology. Cambridge, Mass., 1972.

Nováky, György. *Handelskompanier och kompanihandel: Svenska Afrikakompaniet 1649-1663*. Uppsala, 1990.

Nörregaard, Georg. *Danish Settlements in West Africa, 1658-1850*. Boston, 1966.

—. "Varen til Guinea" in *Handels – og Søfartsmuseel på Kronborg Aarbog*. Helsingør, 1951, 56-66.

—. *Guvernor Edward Carstensens Indberetninger fra Guinea, 1842-1850*. Copenhagen, 1964.

Opoku, Kofi Asare. *West African Traditional Religion*. Singapore, 1978.

Ordbog over Del Danske Sprog. 28 vols.: Copenhagen, 1915-56.

Oxford Universal Dictionary on Historical Principles. 3d. ed.: Oxford, 1955.

Pacheco Pereira, Duarte. *Esmeraldo de Situ Orbis*. trans. and ed. George H.T. Kimble. London, 1937.

Parry, J.H., Philip Sherlock, and Anthony Maingot. *A Short History of the West Indies*. 4th ed.: London, 1987.

Phillips, Thomas. "A Journal of a Voyage made...in 1693, From England ...to Africa" in Awnsham and John Churchill, comps., *A Collection of Voyages and Travels*. 6 vols.: London, 1746.

Postma, Johannes Menne. *The Dutch in the Atlantic Slave Trade, 1600-1815.* Cambridge, 1990.

Rask, Johannes. *En kort og sandferdig Reise-Beskrivelse til og fra Guinea (1708-1713).* Trondheim, 1754.

Ratelband, K. *Vijf dagregisters van het Kasteel São Jorge da Mina aan de Goudkust (1645 – 1647).* The Hague, 1953.

Reindorf, Carl Christian. *The History of the Gold Coast and Asante.* Basel 1895/Accra, 1966.

Reindorf, J. *Scandinavians in Africa: Guide to Materials Relating to Ghana in the Danish National Archives*, ed. J. Simensen. Oslo, 1980.

Römer, Ludewig Ferdinand. *Tilforladelig Efterretning om Kysten Guinea.* Copenhagen, 1760.

Röding, Johann Hinrich. *Allgemeines Wörterbuch der Marine.* Hamburg, 1793-98.

Roggeveen, Arent and Jacob Robijn. *The Burning Fen*, second part, Amsterdam, 1687.

Speith, Jakob. *Die Ewe-Stämme.* Berlin, 1905.

Steward, John Q. and Newton L. Pierce. *Marine and Air Navigation.* Boston, 1944.

Thornton, John. *Africa and Africans in the Making of the Atlantic World, 1400-1680.* Cambridge, 1992.

Van Dantzig, Albert. *Forts and Castles of Ghana.* Accra, 1980.

—. "English Bosman and Dutch Bosman: a Comparison of Texts." *HA* 2-11 (1975-84).

—. "The Akanists: A West African Hausa" in *West African Economic and Social History: Studies in Memory of Marion Johnson*, ed. David Henige and T.C. McCaskie. Madison. 1990, 205-16.

Van den Sleen, W.G.N. *A Handbook on Beads.* Liège, 1967.

Villault, Nicolas de Bellefond. *Relation des Costes d'Afrique, ap-*

pellées Guinée. Paris, 1669. Vogt, John. *Portuguese Rule on the Gold Coast, 1469-1682.* Athens, GA, 1979.

Ward, W.E.F. *A History of Ghana.* London, 1969.

Westergaard, Waldemar. *The Danish West Indies under Company Rule, 1671-1745.* New York, 1917.

Wilks, Ivor. "The Rise of the Akwamu Empire, 1650-1710." *Transactions of the Historical Society of Ghana* 3 (1957): 99-136.

Zook, George Frederick. "The Company of Royal Adventurers Trading into Africa." *Journal of Negro History* 4, no. 2 (1919): 134–231.

AAkjær, Svend. *Maal og Vægt.* Copenhagen, 1936.

INDEX

Page references are those of Tilleman's pagination [-].

A

Abenny/Ebenny [Abaine] 52, 54
Abrahambu [Abrem] 77
abyss [The Bottomless Pit] 48
Acania/Accany/Akania/Acanies 115, 116, 118, 119
Acara [Accra] 5, 86, 87, 88, 93, 94, 98, 99, 100, 103, 116, 119, 127, 129, 135, 152, 155 poor anchoring ground, 156
Accoda see Forts/lodges
Ado, Prince Regent of Akwamu 104-06, 108
Adra 83
Adumb [Adom] 116
Agia [Egya] 79, 83
Adels-Burser 57, 66, 75, 90
Akim ix
Akwamu, see also *Qvambu,* viii-xi
Albrecht, Henning, Governor at Frederiksborg 91
Amacrofu [Amamfro] 77
Am amforé [Amanful/Danish Mount] 77, 78
ambergris 5, 152
Amppeny 68
Anemobu [Anomabu] lodges 71, 79, 81
Angola i
animals: boars 13; buffaloes 13; deer 9, 14, 158; elephants 13; monkeys 14, 160; *Steen-Bukke* 9, 142, 158; domestic animals 141-42, 157; wild animals 142
d'Annobou [Annabon) 157
Anteen reef 60
Antwerp v
Aprag [Little Accra] 90
Arder [Allada] 99, 112, 127, 130
Arf, Nicolaus Janssen ix-x, 95-96
Assené [Assini] 50, 51, 54
Attreba 60

85

Axim i, v

B

Badu 31
Baffa Setterna 29
Baixos [Shoais of St. Ann] 15
Banco weight 120
Barsiar/Bansiar [Bassua, King of Akwamu] 96, 104-05
beads 52, 126, 129 *Agrii*, 150, 153
beans 137
beer 128
Berby 42
beverages as trade wares 52
Bight, of Benin 128, 153, 157; of Biafra i
birds: tame pigeons 142, wild 142, 157, parrots 160
blankets 129
blockade vi-vii
Bodema/Bredva, King of Fetu iv
Bolt, Pieter sold Christiansborg to the Portuguese 95
Borsalo 4
Bording, Claus iv
bossies [cowrie shells] 125, 129, 150
Bottava [Bottowa] 29, 30
Botteru [Butri] 59, 60
Boven Coast 141, 153
Brandenburgers 1, 2, 5, 57, 59
brandy 10, 52, 150
bread 128
Breku [Senya Beraku] 85, 86, 101
buffalo hides 5
Bugubu 4

C

Cabo Corsso see Castles
Apollonia 53, 54; *de Baikos Svino* [Rock Sess Point] 28
Corsso/Carolusberg [Cape Coast Castle] 69, 70, 72, 73, 75, 76, 77, 79, 81, 82, 119; *Lahu* [Grand Lahou] 46, 47, 50, 53; *de Lopo Consalves* [Cape Lopez] 159; *Messuratte/Misserado* [Cape

Mesurado] 6, 19, 21, 22; *de Monte* [Cape Mount] 1-2, 10, 15, 18; *de Palma* [Cape Palmas] 36, 37, 38, 39, 40, 42; *Tagrin* [Tagrin Point] 3, 4, 5; *Tres Puntas* [Cape Three Points] 3, 57; *Verde* 1, 2, 3, 4, 101, 154

Caces 4

Cagranco 4

Cammecovv 4

Caracone 4

Carlof, Henrich v-vi, 70

Carolus-Berg see Castles

Carramanasse [Kwamina Ansa] 66

CASTLES. *Cabo Corsso/Carolusberg* [Cape Coast] 2, 3, 4, 69-70, 72, 73, 75, 76, 77, 79, 81, 82, 119; *Christiansburg* [Christiansborg] 5, 90-92, 95-96, 99, 101; *St. George d'el Mina* [Elmina] 64, 65-68, 69, 77, 79, 90, 119

Catholic 158

Charlotta Amalia, frigate 11-12

cheating in trade: rotten mallagette 39; weighted tusks 54; adulteration of gold 121-22

Christian IV, King of Denmark-Norway iii

Christiansburg see Castles

circumcision 136

civet 5, 9, 152

Claessen, Jan, Dey of Fetu v-vi

cloth; African 5, 153, imported from Europe 5, 9, 10, 51-52, 151 numbers 27 – 37

Comfu 131-32

Commate, "devil worship" 4

Commendo [Komenda] Little and Great 63, 64, 77, 78, 118

Companies: Company of Royal Adventurers (English) 4; East India Company (Danish) 2; Glückstadt Company (Danish) 3, 4, 5; Royal African Company (English) 5; Swedish African, Asiatic and American Trading Company I, 2; West India Company (Dutch) 1, 2, 3, 4; West India-Guinea Company (Danish) 5-6

Compans, Claus pirate 8

Copenhagen ix-x, 156

coral (blood coral) 52, 150

Cormantyn [Kormantin] 79, 82, 83, 85
Cornelissøn, Christen 91-94
"custom" 9
Cramer, Jost vii
Cuteru/Cuteru lahu [Coetroe] 46

D

Danish/Danes i, iv, vi-ix, 18, 70, 73, 75, 81, 90, 91, 95, 99, 104
Dasso 29
De Geer, Louis iv
Denmark-Norway/Denmark i, iii-ix, 14, 74, 95
De Ruyter, Dutch Admiral Michael Adrianzoon viii, 8, 84
Dey see Claessen
Domera 45
Dorvvyn 43, 86
Dutch t *et passim*, 5, 51, 55, 57, 58, 61, 62, 63, 65, 67,71, 72, 73, 74, 79, 83, 89, 103, 127 *Duyvelsberg* [Devil's Mount] 84

E

earthenware mugs 150
Elmina i, v, vii, xi, 65
England/English i, iii-xi, xii, 5, 9, 11, 12, 14, 15, 19, 51, 61, 62, 63, 69, 73, 74, 75, 79, 81, 83, 85, 88, 127, 161
Ennechiannus [Anishan/Biriwa] 79, 80, 81
evil people on Tusk Coast 40

F

Fanlijn [Fante] 81, 116
Fatima 4
Fensman, Nickoiai ix
Fetu iv, vii-xi, 66, 68, 73, 77, 78, 116, 118
Fida [Whydah] 127, 130
fish, *corcobados* 14, *harders* 14, *saphor* 14; at Accra 110, 111, 143-47, shellfish 146
fishing boat on board ship 125, 160, 161, 162
fishing methods 147
fitisseiro [fetish priest] 131-36
fitissie [fetish] 93, 133, personal 134-35

Formosa 4

FORTS/LODGES: *Accoda* [Akwida/Fort Dorothea] 58, 60; *Agia* [Egya] 79, 83; *Anemobu* [Anomabu] 71, 79, 81, 82; Axim 1,3, 55-57, 76; *Bottera* [Butri] Dutch Fort Batenstein 59, 60; *Breku* [Senya Beraku] 85; *Commendo* [Komena] 63-64; *Cormantyn* [Kormantin] 79, 83-84; *Crève-Coeur* 5, 6, 89, 10; *Ennechiannus* [Anashan/Biriwa] 79, 80, 81; *Friderichs-Berg Friderichs-Berg* [Gross Friedrichsburg] 57; *James Castle* [James Fort] 6, 88-89, 101; *Kong* [Mt. Cong] 79;*Nassow* [Nassau] 79-80, 81; *Ogua* 74; Fort Royal, see Fort Fredriksborg; St. Jago 68, 69, 76, 79; *Samma* [Shana] 62; *Secondé* [Secondi] 61; *Takorary* [Takoradi] 60, 71; *Wimba* [Winneba] 86

Frederik III, King of Denmark-Norway ii, vii

French/France i, v, 2, 3, slave raid 18, 51, 127

Friderichs-Berg see Forts/lodges

fruits/edible plants: in gardens 56; *cassu* [cashew] 56; citrons 9, 56, 138; coconuts 56; grain 111; oranges 56, 138-39; *patattas* 139; pawpaws 9, 139-40, 157; pineapples 56, 139-40; plantains/bananas 55, 139; plums 140; (Spanish) pepper 140; pomegranates 56; sugar cane 139; *turreba* [garden eggs] 140; *water-limoner* [?passion fruit] 56; yams 139

G

Galinhos 10

Galrivoy/Grova [?Growa Point] 40

gardens: at Axim 56; at Fort Frederiksborg 76

gold i, iii, vi, 10, 53, 54, 56, 59, 60, *kakra* gold 61, 62, 64, 84, 95, 115, 116, acquisition 116-18; nuggets 116; adulteration 64, 119, 121-22; weights 120; 152; Gold Coast 1 ff., 50, 54, 98, 99, 115, 121, 122 126, 127, 129, 153, 156; gold trade: at Assini 51; at Akwida 59; at Butri 60; at Takoradi 61; at Secondi 62; at Komenda 64;

good people at Grand Lahou 47; at Apollonia 54

Grand Setter [Grand Sesters] 34, 35, 38

Greenland iii

Greyn Coast 23, beginning of 26; end of 38; 157

guns/gunpowder 12, 22, 52, 64, 69, 84, 89, 90, 97, 129, 150

H

harmattan [*Armetan*] 156
Hennique, King of Fetu vii
hats as trade wares 52, 151
Henricksøn, Daniel a Danish sailor 21
Hesperides 154
hides 4, 152
Holland/Hollander vi, 59
Holmes, Captain Robert vii-viii, xii

I

Iceland iii
Ile 4
interlopers 1
Ile de Prince [Principe] 157
ivory/elephant teeth/tusks 1, 4, 9, 10, 19, 21, 25, 42, 44, 45, 47, 54, 152, 160; "sea cow" [hippopotamus] tusks 152, 160

J

Juel, Jens x
John the Second, King of Portugal 66

K

Karl X Gustav, King of Sweden iv
Killigrevv, Commendeur 12
Kocks Brød [Cook's Loaf/Dampa Hill] 87, 100
Kong [Mt. Cong] 78, 79
Kongens Plats [King's town on River Cess] 27
Kramer, Joseph, Governor at Fort Frederiksborg 74-75; see also Cramer

L

Labbadee [Labadi] 97-98, 110
Lygaard, Erik x
Lykke, Governor Hans viii, 75

M

Madrebomba 10
mallaget [pepper] 25, 39, 138
mats 5, 9, 152, 160
metal wares brought from Europe 5, 9, 52, 149, 150
Melville, Governor Isaac 70
Meyer, Hartwig ix
millie 136-37
mirrors 150
Moth, Mathias x
Mourée [Mori] 80, 81, 82, 83

N

names carved on a stone 7-8, on a tree 8
Nassow see Forts/lodges
Netherlands i, iii, viii
Nungo [Nungua] 98, 101, 110, 156
Nurse, Henry viii
nuts; cashew 56; coconut 141, 157; kola 140; palm nuts 141; tiger nuts [*acrossa*] 138

O

oil palm 141
Ostras 4
Osu 5 See also *Ursoe*
oysters 8

P

palmwine 9, 121, 141
Paniha 10
Pensado, Governor Tobias 74
Petersen, Harding ix
Petit Diepen 24
Piedras 4
piracy: 5, French 3; English 11-12
Pitero 42
Popo, 127, 130

Port Dale [Portudal] 4
Porta 4
Portugal i, viii, 66
Portuguese 2, 3, 13, 15, 17, 25, driven out of Axim 51; 55, 66, driven out of Elmina 67; bought and returned Christiansborg Castle 95; 127, 131, 157, castle on São Thomé 158-59
Prince-Eylandt [Parrot Island] 159-60
Punte Legard 4

Q

Qvaqva Coast 40, 46-49, 50, 157
Qvambu [Akwamu] 86, 87, occupy *Christiansborg Castle* 96; 98, 102-03, 104-06, 108, Akwamu king's privileges 106-08; occupations in Akwamu/Accra 109-115; wage war 113-14; 136

R

Rahala, name or title of a king 17
redwood 5, 19, 24, 152
religion 4, 12-13
reptiles and insects 14, 148-49
Rensang Sasaraku [Ansa Sasraku, King of Akwamu] 104
Riaven/Griaven/Goyan [?Garroway Point] 35, 38
rice 5, 9, pegla 12, 19; best at Cape Mesurado 21; 138, 152, 157
RIO/RIVER: *Corse* 24; *Cumba* 24; *Gambia* 3, 4, 5, 152; *Gabon* 159; *de Nuno* 4; *Pogona* 4; *del Punto* 23; *St. Andreas* 42, 43, 44, 45; *St. Jean* 23, 24, 26, 39; *St. Paulo* 18; *de Sester* 25, 26, 29; *Sierra Liona* 2, 5, 6-7, 10, 154, 159, 160; *de Sveria Costa* 48, 50; *Svinko* 22, 23; *de Volta* 5, 99, 127
Roo Cleven [red cliffs] 45
Ruyters, see De Ruyter

S

Sabatra 45
Sabrabon [Blubar] 30
Sabu [Asebu] 77, 78, 80, 116, 118
sacrifice/sacrificing 132, 133, 134
St. Anna 4
St. George d'el Mina see Castles

St. Pedro 4, 24
St. Thomas 12
St./São Thomé 1, 25, 153, 157, 158
salt 110-1, 152
Samma [Shama] 62
Sangvin 29
Satan/Devil 4, 12-13, 131, 136
Schmidt, Samuel 3, 71
Secondé 61
Serbera 10
Sester (Little) 28
Setter and Cru [Settra Kru] 30, 31, 33-34, 38
Setterna 29
Ships: *Bachelor's Delight* 5; *Charlotta Amalia* 5, 11-12; *Christiansborg* 5; *Gyldenløwe's Vaaben* 154; *Havmanden* 18; *Københavns Børs* xviii; *Laurvigen* 154; *Ny Københavns Vaaben* 154; *Stockholm Slott* 3; confiscated 4, 5; trust no ship 159,
Sierra Liona 6-7, 8, 9-14, 15, 155
silver 122
Sioco [Sokko] 89
Sitro 42
Slave Coast viii, 122, 128
slave trade: 1, partitioning and provisioning of ships 123-25; staff and crew 125; wares for purchase 125-26, see also trade wares; merchant on board 126-27; 153 slaves: 1, 2; acquisition and raids 18, 130-31; 135, 153
Souvalle 4
Spain i
Spanish Cavalry, a stand of trees 88
sugar 153
sugar revolution 1
Svino 28
Swede/Swedes/Swedish/Sweden i-v, 70, 71, 91
Sweru, Nicholas, General Director at Elmina 90
swimming 49

T

Tabo/Tabotré [Tabu] 41

Tabo de Gravv 24
Tabokanen [Buchanen] 25, 26
Tabodue 41
Taho 42
Takorary [Takoradi] lodges 60, 71
tallow 52, 150
Tebu (Tobo) 53, 54
Terre Peckenina 64
Tessie [Teshi] 51, 98, 99, 100, 110, 155, 156
Thorsøn/Thors, Thomas 5, 11
Tiebe-lahu 48
tobacco, Portuguese 5; 150; pipes 150
trade wares: at Rio Gambia 4-5; 46, 51-52, from Europe 149-52; purchased in Africa 152-53 trading practices: trade begins at Cape Mesurado 5-6; trustworthy traders 13; come aboard ship 9,10, 39, 49; send smoke signals 17; untrustworthy traders 20; 21, 23, 24, 27, 29, 31, 32, 34, 39; cheating 39, 42, 54; trade at night 56-57; 64, at Accra 112-3; in gold trade 119-20; from ships 121; changing tastes 126, carrying trade 153; at River Gabon 161
Trane, Johan ix
Tranquebar iii
travat [line squall] 16, 44, 112, 155, 138, 155
troy weight 120
Tuesday, holy day 134
Tusk Coast 40, 46, 54, 157
tusks, see Ivory

U

Ugva [Ogua] 74
Ursoe [Osu] 71, 97, 110

V

Van Houssen, Director General Casper vi-vii
Von Krustenstjerna, Johan Philip iv
Vos/Voss, Anthonie vi, 71

W

Wappa 31, 34, 38
war: Akwamu against Accra 103-04; 109, 114; during *travat* time 113-14; Accras against Slave Coast peoples 129-30; 160
water and wood supplies: best at Sierra Leone 5; 9, 11, 17, 27, 32, 33, 35, 36, 37, 44, 158, at the Gabon River 159
wax 47, 152, 160
weapons (hand): assegais 12; bows and arrows 12, 17; daggers 12
West Indies iii, x, 12
Wetu 48
White Rock 28
Wimba [Winneba] 86

Z

Zabuya, Admiral Diego [d'Azambuja] 66

NOTES

1 The union of Denmark and Norway was established in 1380, and continued unbroken until 1814. During certain periods Norway had virtually provincial status. The seat of government was always at Copenhagen.

2 Blake (1977), 24, 42-53; Vogt (1979), 14-15.

3 Blake (1977), 106-37; Vogt (1979), 78, 92.

4 Davies (1957), 9-10; Daaku (1970), 9-10; Blake (1977), 138.

5 Davies (1957), 8; Fage (1969), 66.

6 Nörregaard (1966), 8-20; Justesen (1980), 310-17; Nováky (1990), 76-80, 240, 244-45.

7 Jones (1985), 1-11.

8 Nörregaard (1966), 21-22; Justesen (1980), 338-22; Feldbæk (1981), 152-55.

9 Daaku (1970), 153-55; Van Dantzig (1980), 41-43.

10 Nörregaard (1966), 7, 11-15; Justesen (1980), 311-12.

11 See Chapter 5, note 33.

12 Nörregaard (1966), 17.

13 Ibid., 18.

14 Ibid.; Jones (1983), 144 n32.

15 Nörregaard (1966), 19-20.

16 See Chapter 5.

17 Nörregaard (1966), 32.

18 Nörregaard (1966), 60-61; Justesen (1980), 338.

19 See Chapter 1, note 17.

20 Nörregaard (1966), 60-61; Justesen (1980), 349. Juel and Moth were two of the men to whom Tilleman dedicated his work.

21 Ehrencron-Müller (1930), 263; J. Reindorf (1980), 124.

22 Jones (1983), 4 n7. Also Jones' translation of Wilhelm Johann Müller *Die afrikanische auf den guineischen Gold Cust gelegene Landscbaft Fetu*, Hamburg 1673 in Jones (1983), 134-259.

23 Robijn/Roggeveen *The Burning Fen*, second part, 1687, reprinted 1971. This is a collection of sea charts whose title is a play on words by the cartographer himself. It is a literal translation of the Dutch name "Roggeveen," and suggests the fires lit on land to guide ships at sea.

24 Throughout, Tilleman's designation of latitude agrees closely with those of his contemporaries, such as Barbot, and modern sources, such as *Africa Pilot*. He employed no longitudinal designations. Until the appearance of accurate chronometers, meridians varied: one, established in 1494 by Spain and Portugal, was 370 leagues west of Cape Verde; another, established in 1634, was the Ferrömeridian, 20° west of the Paris observatory. Barbot cited the meridian of Tenerife (1992, 38).

25 Actually, the Portuguese were active on the Guinea coast from the mid-1440s. See Fage (1969), 51 ff.; Blake (1977), 5-6; Vogt (1979), 5. Tilleman's "1481" was probably a slightly mistaken dating referring to the building of Elmina Castle in 1482. For the beginning of the Guinea Coast at Sierra Leone, see Barbot (1992), 231, 233 n1, Villault (1669), 1, has it starting at Cape Verde.

26 However, Phillips, an Englishman, (1746), 200-04, went ashore at St. Jago, was a guest of the governor, and traded there.

27 Presumably Tilleman was calculating in sea miles: one sea mile=7.5 km. Villault (1669), 45; Fage (1969), 70-73; for French forts on Gorée Island off Cape Verde, see Barbot (1992), 44ff. For a contrast to Tilleman's impressions see Rask's report written about his stay there in 1709, remarking on the French hospitality but confirming their strict control of trade. Rask (1754), 6-16. I have been unable to find anything about Claus Bording. For the English fort on James Island see Lawrence (1963), 250-53.

28 Almost all these places are found on the Robijn/Roggeveen maps. See Appendix. For villages see Barbot (1992), 219.

29 The closest I have found to the term *Commaté* is *Jan Commé/Jan Compon* in Jones (1983), 271. For a discussion of names of the deity, see ibid. 176 nl56. On religion see Villault (1669), 82-83; Barbot (1992), 221-22.

30 For trade wares see Villault (1669), 59; Barbot (1992), 219-20. For redwood, see ibid, 200-01 n22. For perpetuaner or rask see Chapter Five, note 5; Jones (1985), 317. Bracelets of metal were known by the Portuguese term *manillas*. They were often made of copper in the form of an open ring. *Manggods* signifies a low quality alloy of tin and lead. "Portuguese tobacco" probably means tobacco brought by the Portuguese from Brazil.

31 For this watering place, which he calls Bay of France, see Barbot (1992), 184.

32 *Atlantic Ocean Pilot* (1884), 455 relates that "[t]he entrance of the Sierra Leone is obstructed by an extensive sandbank, interspersed with large stones, named Middle Ground, which in many parte becomes dry at low water. There is a channel on either side of it; and on the south side between the bank and Cape Sierra Leone and Freetown is about a mile in least width, and from 7 to 20 fathoms deep, and is consequently the proper passage into the river; indeed, that to the northward of the bank is only fit for small vessels, and even by them it is but seldom attempted, as they must cross a 9-foot bar which appears to connect the Middle Ground with the flat that fringes the main." See also Roggeveen/Robijn (1971), 14, and Barbot (1992), 181-82 for anchoring in Bay of France at 16 to 18 fathoms. Where Tilleman describes the bottom as red, Barbot writes of yellow sand (ibid., 184). The phrase "standing river" presents another problem in translation. Tilleman may simply be referring to tides and high water at Sierra Leone. See *Africa Pilot* (1967). 17.

33 This rock has been preserved in the Sierra Leone Museum in Freetown: Jones (1985), 182. For Admiral de Ruyter and Captain

Robert Holmes in West Africa see Chapter Five. A rock in the sea off the Senegal Coast has been named for the pirate Campaen. See Barbot (1992), 48, 65. I have found no mention of the tree in other sources.

34 *Cabusee/caboceiro/capucheer/kabossie* is derived from the Portuguese *caboceiro* head man. The term was used generally by all the Europeans.

35 *A fjerding-vei* =about 1.9 km. A chief or "Captain" by the name of Jan Thomas was mentioned by Villault (1669), 64, 68. See also Jones (1985), 24. In 1678 Jean Thomas was about 70 years old, according to Barbot (1992), 184, 186, 187, 210-11. If this is the same man as Tilleman's Thomisse he would have been about 90 years old at their meeting, a fact which would certainly have evoked comment from Tilleman. This man might then be a successor/namesake.

36 For trade wares see Villault (1669), 86-87; knives as an important item, Jones (1985), 114; for the demand for metals and metal products see Hair (1989), 13-14. See also Barbot (1992), 219-20, 225 n4; Chapter Eleven for a list of trade wares. Civet is a thick yellowish musky-odored substance found in a pouch near the sexual organs of the civet cat and used in perfume. *Fyrstaal* refers to steel used for striking a flint.

37 On the English at Sierra Leone see Hemmersam in Jones (1983), 100-01; Villault (1669), 63, 87; Davies (1957), 214-15. Tilleman's reference to the English station "inland" must be the fort in the estuary on Bunce/Bence Island, built in 1672. Barbot (1992), 182, 196-98; Davies (1957), 219-20; Lawrence (1963), 42; Fage (1969), 73.

38 See Appendix, Roggeveen/Robijn maps.

39 For Thomas Thorsøn/Thors see Nørregard (1966), 56. The *Charlotte Amalia* was siezed by the pirates/buccaneers John Cook, Ambrose Cowley, Edward Davis, the doctor Lionel Wafer, and William Dampier aboard the *Revenge,* Originally named after Christian V's queen, the *Charlotte Amalia* was renamed *Bachelor's Delight,* a name more fitting to its purpose

and crew. She then embarked on a far more extensive journey than the one Tilleman described, sailing along the east coast of South America, around Cape Horn and up the west coast as far as Panama, back again around Cape Horn, and northwards. In the spring of 1688, after five dramatic years around South America, the ship reached the Caribbean and disappeared. Not only is Tilleman's account at fault, but his date, 1693, is wrong. All records of the dates of launching, the last journey of the *Charlotte Amalia*, and the journals of the captain and officers on the *Revenge* and *Bachelor's Delight* indicate the correct year to be 1683. Tilleman's date could very possibly have been a printer's error. From the description of the ship, its condition and size, and the details of its capture, there can be no doubt that the *Bachelor's Delight* was in fact the *Charlotte Amalia*. There appear to be no records of the fate of the Danish crew. For a description of the *voyages* undertaken, see Bredsdorff "Fregatten Charlotta Amalia's Mærkelige Skæbne" *Arbog1975 af Selskabet Handels – og Søfartsmuseets Venner*, Helsingør, 22-41. See also Dampier (1968), xxxii-xxxiii, where Sir Albert Gray, in his introduction, declares this "an act of piracy so flagrant, committed against a friendly nation . . . that Dampier is evidently ashamed to mention it."

40 There are various names in the local languages that could readily result in the term *pegla*, e.g., Sherbro *pɛλɛ* Tonko Limba *paga* (Adam Jones, personal communication).

41 On the character of the people at Sierra Leone, see Brun in Jones (1983), 79; Hemmersan, ibid., 99-102. Barbot (1992), 186 made short shrift of them by declaring all of them "rogues and rebels."

42 For fish see Chapter Ten.

43 Remarkably, Tilleman gives no advice on how to avoid the shoals or what to do in the event one comes into them.

See *Africa Pilot* (1967), 378; Barbot (1992), 223-24, 230-31n16. Tilleman's picture of trade between Sierra Leone and Cape Mount is not quite accurate. The trading was not only with small ships. The English had a lodge at York Island at Sherbro. See Barbot (1992), 236-37. For navigability for large ships in the river he called Sherbro, but which was actually Bum-Kittam-Waanje, see ibid., 250 n16. For the purchase of the chief wares, camwood/redwood and ivory, in this area see ibid., 237.

44 *Travat/travado* from the Portuguese *trovoado*, thunder storm. Writers frequently referred to these storms, line squalls in modern terminology, as *tornadoes*. De Marees (1987), 9 n4; Villaut (1669), 98, 105 – 06; Barbot (1992) 35 nn16-17, 238; Phillips (1746), 205; Labat (1730), 1:96, 105,106; Isert (1992), 210; *Africa Pilot* (1967), 385-86.

45 For fire signals and smoke signifying the presence of a village see, Villaut (1669), 97, 99; Barbot (1992), 251 n19; Bosman (1705), 478.

46 Brun in Jones (1983), 74; Villault (1669), 112; Labat (1730), 1:105; Jones (1985) 29.

47 The name *Rabala* does not appear in contemporary sources. For a king named Falam Bouré/Fallam-Bouré, see Villault (1669), 101-05; Labat (1730), 1: 99. Perhaps this was a title or the designation of a decent group. See Jones (1983), 75 n185.

48 For kidnapping of Africans by the French, see Jones (1985), 29, 79 n197, 182; Barbot (1992), 239 for kidnapping by "many of the European nations," 313 n39; Rask (1754), 203-04.

49 The original reads *Og ere de paa samme Sted intet for vel at troe*. "They" refers to the king and officials, and I interpret this strange phrase to be read as a *caveat*.

50 *Atlantic Ocean Pilot* (1884), 471-72; *Africa Pilot* (1967), 386-87; Roggeveen/Robijn (1971) 17; Barbot (1992), 238.

51 Tilleman gives the impression here that it was only the English who were interested in redwood, but it is listed in subsequent chapters as a trade article for the Danes as well. Ulsheimer in Jones (1983), 26, 26 n28; Barbot (1992), 200-01, 237, 240; Labat (1730), 106. Phillips, Tilleman's contemporary, visited at the St. Paul River from 23 December 1693 to 4 January

1694 in the company of another English captain. They were received well, well treated, and assured, when they left, that the inhabitants had "a great affection for the English, and as much hatred to the French," and that sons would be named for the two captains. Phillips (1746), 210.

52 Roggeveen/Robijn (1.971), 17; Barbot (1992), 128; Atlantic Ocean Pilot (1884), 471; *Africa Pilot* (1967) 387

53 For the "bad people at Mesurado see Villault (1669), 116; Barbot (1992), 239. However, Phillips (1746), 207, found them "civil and courteous."

54 For rice at Mesurado see Villault (1669), 123; Phillips (1746), 207; Labat (1730), 133-34; Jones (1985), 30-31, 32.

55 For arming small boats see Villault (1669). 116-17; Labat (1730 1:131; Jones (1985), 30-31.

56 Tilleman is describing what is now known as Saddle Hills. See Roggeveen/Robijn (1971), 17; *Africa Pilot* (1967), 391. See also De Marees (1987), 13; Villault (1669), 128; Barbot (1992) 240, 253n27; Jones (1985), 30-31.

57 *The Greyn,* or Pepper Coast, the modem Liberia, is "a mountainous country the surface falling south-westerly from the divide of the River Niger basin to a strip of comparatively level land bordering the Atlantic. The coast is low and sandy to marshes and grassy plains. There are patches of high ground. The country in general is covered by extremely dense forest, and the mountains are thickly wooded up to their summits, reported to attain an altitude of over 5,000 ft." *Africa Pilot* (1967), 19.

58 The *Greyn/Malagueta/Manigette/Pepper* Coast derives its name from the main trade article *Aframomum granum paradisi.* Dalziel (1955), 470. There have been various opinions regarding the beginning of Grain Coast; De Marees (1987), 14, Cape Verde; Villault (1669), 39, 132, 145, divides the area into Pepper Coast beginning at the River Cess and the Grain Coast at the River Sanguin; Barbot (1992), map, figure 11, opts for the

River Cess, as does Labat (1730), 147. For all the variations see Ratelbaad (1953), lxxviii, 16 n1. For *Rio Iunk* (Junk) with *Rio del Punto* see the map figure 11 in Barbot (1992).

59 The three mountains may be Table Mountain and the Bassa Hills, which are visible at 30 miles in clear weather. *Africa Pilot* (1967), 391. Rio Corse is now River *St. John; Petit* Dieppe is stated as an alternative toponym to Rio Cors; Tabo Dagrou was explained as the native name for River Cess. For a discussion of the toponyms see Barbot (1992), 154-55 n31.

60 For anchorage at St. John River see *Africa Pilot* (1967), 391.

61 For *Tabo Canee* see Roggeveen/Robijn (1971), 17. This could have been at the site where the modern port Buchanan lies at Tabokanni point. *Africa Pilot*, 393-95.

62 "double land" meant a stretch of coast where. one could see a second layer of land, as it were, behind the seaboard. See De Marees (1987), 13; Barbot (1992), 293 n1; Bosman (1705), 477. This agrees with the description in note 1.

63 River Cess, alternately Sess, Sestos, Sextos, Sester, derives its name from *cestos*, Portuguese for baskets in which pepper was carried. *Petit Dilps* resembles the toponym *Pedit Dispo* for a small village mentioned by Dapper (1670), 338.

64 For Cestos Reef see Barbot (1992), 264, 279 n2; *Africa Pilot* (1967), 397.

65 For anchoring at River Cess see Pacheco Pereira (1937), 109; Roggeveen/Robijn (1971), 17; Barbot (1992), 275; Labat (1730), 149; *Africa Pilot* (1967), 397; Jones (1985), 34, 184.

66 For accounts of the village where the king lived see Villault (1669), 133, 138; Barbot (1992), 265-68; Bosman (1705), 480; Labat (1730), 151; Jones (1985), 34. Phillips (1746) 211 places the village eight miles upriver, and he had been informed that the people there were "very treacherous and bloody." Could rival traders have spread negative propaganda to keep the "good trade" and "good people" to themselves?

67 *Baixa* is the Portuguese term for shoals. *Cabo de Baikos Svino* is the modern Rock Sess Point. Barbot (1992), 279 n2. For the rock resembling a sailing ship see De Marees (1987), 13-14; Barbot (1992), 289; Phillips (1746), 211; Bosman (1705), 483; *Africa Pilot* (1967), 398.

68 For the approach and trade at Sangwin see De Marees (1987), 14; Villault (1669), 145-48, describing only landing and a visit with the king and his brother; Barbot (1992), 289, 194 n3; Bosman (1705), 483-84, anchored but achieved little trade; Labat (1730), 160-61, 163-64; Jones (1985), 34. See also *Africa Pilot* (1967), 399.

69 *Baffa* is Baffu Point; *Setterna* represents no modern village; *Dasso* is possibly the modern Tassu. See Barbot (1992), 294 n5. De Marees (1987), 14, declared this a good place to trade. Neither Barbot nor Bosman anchored but only sailed slowly by Barbot (1992), 289; Bosman (1705), 485.

70 "*Croe* is easey to be knowne by the high naked trees, shewing like a passel of stript Ships whereof you see the beare masts . . ." Roggeveen/Robijn (1971), 19. The simile would be natural and commonplace to sailors, and Tilleman's use of the same one does not necessarily mean he copied or plagiarized, albeit he was certainly using this source.

71 Barbot (1992), 290; *Africa Pilot* (1967), 403, describes the area as having sandy beach "interrupted by Kufuer at Devil's Cliff, a rocky projection about 19m. 8cm. high."

72 For Wappo see De Marees (1987), 14; Villault (1669), 149-50; Barbot (1992), 290, 295n7; Bosman (1705), 486. For a ledge of rocks off Wappi Point and a large rock known as Flat Islet or Totwarrah see *Africa Pilot* (1967), 478. See also Jones (1985), 34. Roggeveen/Robijn (1971), 19 places *Badoe* east of *Wappa*, "Coming before *Wappo*, there lyeth the greatest Cliff of all the *Greyn Coast*, liking unto an Island but not very high above water and flatt, neare it lye yet a multitude of little cliffs lying as well under as above the water."

73 Villault (1669), 155-58, reports that Grand Sesters was called

Grand Paris, and Petit Setter (Tilleman's *Setter*), was called Petit Paris. See also De Marees (1987), 14; Labat (1730), 164. For a discussion of the persistent claim that the French had preceded the Portuguese as discoverers of Guinea (Labat's date is 1366), see Barbot (1992), xi, 290-91, 295 n8. The rock just outside of the town may be Carpenter Rock, *Africa Pilot* (1967), 410.

74 *Riaven/Griaven/Goyann* is probably Garraway Point and River. *Africa Pilot* (1967), 411-12. See also De Marees (1987), 14 n6; Villault (1669), 146; Roggeveen/Robijn (1971), 20. For a round hill see Barbot (1992), 291.

75 For entering the Garraway River see *Africa Pilot* (1967), 411.

76 Villault (1669), 162-63; Barbot (1992), 291-92, 296 n10, locates Cape Palmas at 4°5' N. See also Phillips (1746), 212; Bosman (1705), 486; Africa Pilot (1967), 414 – 15.

77 The dry season prevails here January-April. The harmattan occurs at times, strong winds are rare and brief, as are line squalls, which occur in connection with the rainy season. For coastal currents and winds during these months see *Africa Pilot* (1967), figures B39 and C40. See also Labarthe (1803), 216 n12; Tilleman, chapter 12. Barbot (1992), 293 mentions that maniguette is harvested in January.

78 Ulsheimer in Jones (1983), 20; Brun in ibid., 77-80; Villault (1669), 171.

79 The coastline of Ivory Coast is of two distinct types, the western region being high and rocky, the eastern low and sandy. In the western region the land rises immediately behind the coast and a series of red cliffs, dramatically striped with red and white crevices, is seen east of Kosso, at a height of 45 meters. The red cliffs extend from Sassandra to Fresco. At Grand Lahou the lagoon coast starts and extends eastward for about 90 kilometers. The southern part of the country is forested, *Africa Pilot* (1967), 429, 431. For dangerous surf as a hindrance to landing of passengers and goods, see ibid., 417.

80 *Atlantic Ocean Pilot* (1884), 481; *Africa Pilot* (1967), 414-15.

See Pacheco Pereira (1937), 116; Ulsheimer in Jones (1983), 20, 21 n6; Villault (1669), 178; Roggeveen/Robijn (1971), 20; Labat (1730), 174-75; Jones (1985), 34; Bosman (1705), 487; Barbot (1992), 299.

81 *Galrivoy,* or *Grova,* two miles east of Cape Palmas is probably Growa Point, *Atlantic Ocean Pilot* (1884), 479; *Africa Pilot* (1967), 417. See also *Crova* in Villault (1669), 164; *Growa* in Barbot (1992), 298 for the beginning of the Ivory Coast, 306 nl; *Grua* in Labat (1730), 180.

82 *Tabodue/Tabbo Dune* is probably Half Kavalli, near Kavalli Point. *Africa Pilot* (1967), 418, 420; Barbot (1992), 298. Roggeveen/Robijn (1971), 20, report anchoring depths at 21 and 22 fathoms here, in contrast to Tilleman's 12 or 14.

83 For the rock and anchoring see Barbot (1992), 298.

84 *Taho* [Tahou], *Petero* [Petry], *Sitro* [?], *Berby* [Béréby]. See Barbot (1992), 297.

85 For a description of the Hautes Terres de Drewin see *Africa Pilot* (1967), 426, 427. See also Roggeveen/Robijn, (1971), 21; Bosman (1705), 487; Barbot (1992), 307 n6.

86 For comments on the people see Bosman (1705), 488-89.

87 Villault (1669), 172-74; Barbot (1992), 299, 308n8; Labat (1730), 183-84; *Africa Pilot* (1967), 427-29. Roggeveen/Robijn (1971), 21 sets the course of the river "north west by west and the other north west."

88 For red cliffs see note 1 above; Pacheco Pereira (1937), 115; Barbot (1992), 299; Phillips (1746), 212; Bosman (1705), 489-90.

89 See Barbot (1992), 309 nl5 for Domera and 310 nnl6,17 for Coetroe. See also Phillips (1746), 212.

90 The Quaqua Coast was considered by some to extend from Grand Lahou to Assini, and by others to Cape Three Points. Barbot (1992), 310n17. The term "quaqua" is said to have come from the greeting which the Africans shouted to the arrivals. For an etymological view, see Jones (1983), 20-21n5. For wares

traded at the Quaqua Coast see Villault (1669), 181-82; Labat (1730), 109-12; Jones (1983), 64n116; Jones (1985), 36. On *quaqua* cloth used in the carrying trade—to other parts of the Guinea coast—see Ratelband (1953), xcv; Barbot (1992), 301, 312 n32; Phillips (1746), 213; Daaku (1970), 6, 24; Jones (1983), 64n116.

91 For double land note that *Africa Pilot* (1967), 431, remarks that it is possible to see coconut trees on the shore and forest inland. Today there is a village called Grand Jack 44 kilometers east of Grand Lahou, and another, more important, village called Jacqueville 12 kilometers east of Grand Jack: ibid., Tilleman's *Tiebe-lahu* might be a misprint for *Jacke la Hou*, see Barbot (1992), 311n21.

92 For Wetu see Barbot (1992), 300, 311n22. The Bottomless Pit is a submarine canyon at Abidjan harbor. "From about 15 miles from land it turns toward the coast in a funnel shape, narrowing considerably as it approaches land. At a mile from the shore the channel is scarcely a quarter of a mile wide; at a third of a mile there are still 100 fathoms; and finally, at the head of this singular submarine valley there are 20 fathoms water at the very head of the beach." *Atlantic Ocean Pilot* (1884), *486. See* also Roggevven/Robijn (1971), 21; *Africa Pilot* (1967), 431-32. For *Rio de Sveria de Costa* see Barbot (1992), 3lln24, for the guess that it might be the River Komoè, but *Africa Pilot* (1967), 437, speaks of a Barre Costa, and *Atlantic Ocean Pilot* (1884), 486, lists the River Costa. See also Baesjou (1988), 16. Roggeveen/Robijn (1971), 21, at the Rio de Suero de Costa notes "a cliff upon the Strand, being the first Cliff of all the *Bad-bad* Coast" (my emphasis). This is the term used to describe the foregoing Tusk Coast (*Costa de Malegens*), whereas the Quaqua Coast was that of the "good people" (*Costa de Bonnegens*), so indicated on Roggeveen's maps as well.

93 Swimming was an activity which impressed the early visitors to Africa. Since it was decidedly not a practice among sailors and fisherman in northern Europe (perhaps because the water was too cold), it excited comment from nearly all of them, but few as exaggerated as Tilleman's. See De Marees (1987), 187;

Bosman (1705), 491; Rask (1754), 205.

94 To his credit Tilleman refrained from repeating the claim that the people of the Quaqua Coast were cannibals, to which their pointed teeth were said to bear witness. See Ulsheimer in Jones (1983), 21; Phillips (1746), 213; Bosman (1705), 437.

95 The coast of Ghana is generally of low, sandy beach varied by small bays and rocky headlands. In the extreme west and east, sand spits enclose large lagoons bordered by mangrove forests. *Africa Pilot* (1967), 22. The coast of Ghana can be divided into three categories: the lagoon coast west of Cape Three Points; the promontory coast between Cape Three Points and Accra; and the delta coast at the mouth of the Volta River. Boateng (1970), 21.

96 De Marees (1987), 45-46, 55-56; Ulsheimer in Jones (1983), 34-36; idem., (1985), 37-39.

97 The fort at Akwida is Fort Dorothea. Jones (1985), plate 8. At the site of an abandoned Dutch lodge the Brandenburg Company built Fort Dorothea in 1684. The Dutch captured the fort in 1687, but returned it to the Brandenburgers peaceably by a treaty agreed to in Europe, in order to strengthen the alliance between the Netherlands and Brandenburg. Tilleman's description of a cunning invasion during a banquet appears to be a fantasy. See also Barbot (1992), 360 n37; Bosman (1705), 10; Lawrence (1963), 283-87; Van Dantzig (1980), 38-39; Jones (1985), 81-87. See *Atlantic Ocean Pilot* (1884), 488-89, for the ruins of the fort as a landmark.

98 The Swedish Company had a lodge at Butri established by Heinrich Carlof in 1650 but was driven out by the Dutch in 1653, with the help of the local inhabitants. The Dutch built Fort Batenstein there in 1656. The fort was poorly built but was difficult of access due to its position on a high, steep hill. The reason for building it was that the Dutch knew that the inland gold-producing areas were close. Although Tilleman calls it a small lodge without guns it was actually a small fort with bastions and eight guns—guns, however, which were never used

for defense. Dapper (1670), 432; Barbot (1992), 362 n42; Van Dantzig (1980), ix, 25. Bosman (1705), 15-16, remarks on the extent of cheating in the gold trade in that area, dubbing it "the false mint of Guinea". Barbot (1992), 345, writes that the gold at Butri was "quite pure."

99 *Attreba* may be Attaba. Jones (1985), 44-45. The character of the coast changes to reefs and rocks east of Butri. Roggeveen/Robijn (1971), 22: *Atlantic Ocean Pilot* (1884), 490.

100 The rock in front of Takoradi might have been Barracouta rock, *Africa Pilot* (1967), 448. All the European countries had lodges at Takoradi in the seventeenth century, among them the Dutch Fort Witsen. Villault (1669), 190-91; Barbot (1992), 346; Bosman (1705), 20; Daaku (1970), 15, 62; Van Dantzig (1987), ix; Jones (1985), 99-100, 159 n2, For anchoring there *see Atlantic Ocean Pilot* (1884), 491.

101 Barbot (1992), 346, 365 n54; Phillips (1746), 219; Bosman (1705), 18-20; Davies (1957), 224, 249; Lawrence (1963), 79 (the English fort), 337-39 (Fort Orange); Van Dantzig (1980), ix, 36-37; Jones (1985), 320-21.

102 The Dutch Fort Vredenburgh was built in 1689 on the left bank of the Komenda River. The English, with the aid of the remarkable African entrepreneur John Kabes, built a fort on the right bank in 1695. Henige (1977), 6-9. See also Bosman (1705), 27; Van Dantzig (1980), 42-43, who dates the establishment of the fort at 1694.

103 For the reef see *Africa Pilot* (1967), 451. For Terra Pekine see De Marees (1987), 80; Dapper (1670), 434; Roggeveen/Robijn (1971), 24.

104 Hemmersam in Jones (1983), 127-29; Bosman (1705), 42; Van Dantzig (1980), ix. For drawings of Elmina Castle see Ulsheimer in Jones (1983), 22; Hemmersam in Jones (1983), 128; Lawrence (1963), 134, 157, 163, 170-72, plates 1-4a, 7-36.Van Dantzig (1980), 4. See also De Marees (1987), 218-19; Dapper (1670), 435-36.

105 For Dom Diogo d'Azambuja and *Carramanasse*, identified as Kwamina Ansa, see Daaku (1970), 52-53; Van Dantzig (1980), 3. João II of Portugal ascended the throne in 1481 and sent a fleet led by d'Azambuja out at the end of that year. It arrived at Elmina in January 1482 and immediately set about building the fort. Claridge (1964), 1:41-48. See also Pacheco Pereira (1937), 119-20; De Marees (1987), 213; Ratelband (1953), ixv-lxii; Müller in Jones (1983), 141-42; Dapper (1670), 435; Lawrence (1963), 103-07; Blake (1942), 40-44, 73-78; Blake (1977), vii-xx, 98-99, 141-42, 210-11; Hair (1994). For an account of Kwamina Ansa's very real misgivings, and for details of building once he agreed to it, see Vogt (1979), 20-27.

106 For the Dutch takeover of Elmina see Ratelband (1953), lxvii-lxix; Dapper (1670), 436-39; Bosman (1705), 42, who gives the date as 1638; Lawrence (1963), 131ff.; Claridge (1964), 1:92-96, for the Dutch version, and 97-99 for the Portuguese; Daaku (1970), 53-54; Vogt (1979), 189-92; Van Dantzig (1980), 14-17.

107 In fact, the Dutch inflicted little damage to São Jorge/Castle d'el Mina from the hill, and the Portuguese cannons were useless against the Dutch on the hill. A stalemate was the result. It was, rather, a cannonade at close quarters that won the day for the Dutch. Vogt (1979), 191. The fort on St. Jago hill was originally a strong redoubt which was rebuilt in the 1660s and named Coenraadburg. This was the only fort to be built for military reasons alone. Van Dantzig (1980), 16-17. See also Ratelband (1953), lxx; Barbot (1992), 374 n2; Bosman (1705), 46-47; Labat (1730), a drawing following 286; Lawrence (1963), 80-81; Jones (1983), 142. Tilleman's supposition of the name having a connection to the date of the takeover is not correct because the hill already had that name before the battle. See Claridge (1964), 1:101 n1.

108 Elmina, also known in the early sources as the Village of Two Parts, is on the mouth of the river/lagoon Benya/Salt River, and has one of the best natural harbors on the Gold Coast. Ratelband (1953), lxv; Bosman (1705), 46; Blake (1977), 80, 99-100; Van Dantzig (1980), 3; Jones (1983), 339 n2; *Africa Pilot*

(1967), 452. For *Amppeny* see Barbot (1992), 348, who says that it is not large but recommends it as a good place for an establishment. Possibly what Tilleman calls *Amppeny* is Barbot's *la Mina* which could muster "almost 6,000 men bearing arms," Ibid., 370 n7, 373-74. Vogt (1979), 179-81, locates Ampeni west of São Jorge, the village from which the Dutch launched an attack on the castle in 1625. See also Roggeveen/Robijn (1971), map showing Ampenny between two "Salt towns" west of Elmina.

109 At the time of Tilleman's writing, the castle was under control of the Royal African Company, and the office of Agent-General had been displaced by a Council of Three Merchants, to preside in turn. This arrangement was in effect *from* 1687 to l691, after which it was modified by appointing one of the merchants as chairman. The office of Agent-General was revived in 1700. Dalby Thomas was appointed to the post in 1703 and held it for seven years. Davies (1957), 244-45. See also Phillips (1746), 220-21; Bosman (1705), 48-52; Lawrence (1963), 185, 188. For titles see Glossary; Bosman (1705), 99.

110 For the history of Cape Coast Castle see the Introduction. The year of its establishment is given variously as 1652, Müller in Jones (1983), 142; 1653, Van Dantzig, (1980), xi; 1655, Lawrence (1963), 183. See also Nørregaard (1966), 9-10; Van Dantzig (1980), 23-24; Nováky (1990), 239-46.

111 For Carlof's career, see Donnan (1930), 1:98-99; Nørregaard (1966), 9, 10, 15-19, 21, 25. 27; Daaku (1970), 62; Van Dantzig (1980), 23-25, 28-29; Jones (1983), 144 n31; Law (1991), 27. For Schmidt's surrender of the fort see Jones (1983), 144 n32.

112 The "cunning" exercised by the Fetu was their entering the fort while the Swedish director was out in the fields. For the seesawing ownership—Fetu-Swedish-Fetu-Dutch—see Nørregaard (1966), 18-20; Daaku (1970), 16-17, 62-63, 90-91, 109-11; Müller in Jones (1983), 145-46n39; Zur Eich in ibid., 262-64; Nováky (1990), 143-45.

113 For the background of Holmes' journey to West Africa see Zook (1919), 42-55.

114 Bosman (1705), 48, 50-51; Müller in Jones (1983), 139-40, 251; *Atlantic Ocean Pilot* (1884), 494-95; *Africa Pilot* (1967), 453.

115 For Joos/Jost Cramer, another former employee of the Dutch West India Company, and his agreement with the leaders of Fetu for the construction of Frederiksborg, see Nørregaard (1966), 22-23; Van Dantzig (1980), 29; Jones (1983), 362 n8.

116 For descriptions of Frederiksborg see Zur Eich in Jones (1983), 261-62; Villault (1669), 195-97; Barbot (1992), 399-401; Lawrence (1963), 77, 82, 186; Nørregaard (1966), 29, 31-33. For an engraving of Cape Coast Castle and Frederiksborg see Jones (1983), 22.

117 For villages around Fredenksborg see Müller in Jones (1983), 140-41; Barbot (1992), 400: Phillips (1746), 221 describes two gardens at Cape Coast Castle.

118 *Amamforé* was also known as *Amanful, Mount Manfro*, Danish Mount. For the boundaries of Fetu see Müller in Jones (1983), 138-39; Dapper (1760), 434; Bosman (1705), 47; map in Van Dantzig (1980), 89.

119 Fetu was eventually absorbed by the Fante. Jones (1983), 136-40, 146, 154-55; Bosman (1705), 47-48; Davies (1957), 41, 278, 282, 283; Nørregaard (1966), 22ff; Daaku (1970), 91, 108-11.

120 Barbot (1992), 413 n2; Bosman (1705), 53.

121 For the unsuitable architecture and "foul stagnant air," at Fort Nassau see Van Dantzig (1980), 13.

122 De Marees (1987), 81-83; Brun in Jones (1983), 78-90; Ratelband (1953), ixx-ixxi; Müller in Jones (1983), 249; Barbot (1992), 412-13, plate 36; Bosman (1705), 54-55; Lawrence (1963), 85, 242-44; Daaku (1970), 12, 14, 47; Postma (1990), 17 – 18. For anchoring at Mori Point, with a ruined fort as a landmark, see *Africa Pilot* (1967), 453-54; also Barbot (1992), 413-14 n4.

123 For staff at Anashan/Biriwa see Davies (1957), chart, 248, showing only one man at Anashan in 1696-97, 149; Barbot (1992), 420 n4. See also Villault (1669), 206-07; Lawrence (1963),

85; Van Dantzig (1980), xi, 33; Jones (1983), 245 n480.

124 Davies (1957), chart, 257-58 shows a staff of twelve at Anomabu in 1696 and ten in 1697. See also Bosman (1705), 56 – 57; Nørregaard (1966), 26, 27, 28; Van Dantzig (1980), xi, 35, 36, 53, 59. The English built two forts at Anomabu: Fort Charles, 1679-80, and Fort Anomabu 1753. See also Müller in Jones (1983), 144; Barbot (1992), 416-17; Lawrence (1963), 349-51. For the English acquisition of Cape Coast and lodges see Introduction.

125 Davies (1957), chart, 247-48, shows a staff of only two for 1693-96, and none for 1697, the years that Tilleman's text would cover. Egya, like Anashan, was intermittently occupied and evacuated between 1683 and 1713. Ibid., 224, 226, 249. See also Barbot (1992), 417; Van Dantzig (1980), xi, 35, 36.

126 The fortress was Fort Amsterdam. See De Marees (1987), 83-84 n23; Ratelband (1953), lxxxii-iv; Phillips (1846), 226: Barbot (1992), 417-18; Bosman (1705), 57-58; Davies (1957), 9, 25; Lawrence (1963), 245-49; Daaku (1970), 16-17, 47; Van Dantzig (1980), xi, 21-23, 33; Postma (1990), 64 map.

127 For De Ruyter's expedition see Bosman (1705), 58; Zook (1919), 55-57, 65-66; Claridge (1964), 1:111-15.

128 This unsavory report of Devil's *Mount/Duyvels Berg/Monte de Diable* does not appear in other sources. However, De Marees (1987), 84, writes of it as a place of sacrifice; Ratelband (1953), 96 n4; Barbot (1992), 426-27, 427-28 nl; Bosman (l705), 62; Baesjou (1988), 49, and note 155.

129 At Senya Beraku the Dutch had a lodge in mid-seventeenth century, and the English planned to build a fort, using the cannons from Fort Royal, a project which lapsed according to Lawrence (1963), 341. See also Barbot (1992), 428 29 nn6, 7; Van Dantzig (1980), xi, 49-50.

130 Dapper (1670), 447.

131 The Gã (Akras) were in constant conflict with the Akwamu during the early and mid-seventeenth century. In two great battles the Gã were defeated: the first one, in 1677 under the

leadership of Okai Koi, was lost to Akwamu, largely by default when the greater part of the Gã army defected; the second one, in 1680, when the Gã were led by Okai Koi's successor, Ashangmo. See Daaku (1970), 154-55; Wilks (1957), 106, 111. Again, due to internal conflict and dissension among the Gã, the Akwamu were victorious. This resulted in the exodus of many Gã who, under Ashangmo's leadership, settled in Anecho (Little Popo). Thus the Akwamu were the paramount state during the entire period described by Tilleman, and it was to the Akwamuhene that the Europeans had to defer and pay custom. See Bosman (1705), 64-65; Reindorf (1895/1966), 21-22/33-34, 24/36, 59/60-61; Ward (1969), 105-14; Kwamena Poh (1973), 22-25 – For more on the Akwamu rule see Chapter Seven.

132 For some strange reason Tilleman seems to have relocated Winneba, placing it east of Senya Beraku. Roggeveen/Robijn (1971), 24, give the order of appearance, traveling eastward, as Danish Hill, *Biemba, Berku,* Cook's Loaf. Assuming that *Biemba* is identical to *Wimba* (Winneba), it would appear that Tilleman had little or no personal knowledge of these places and had read his charts incorrectly. See De Marees (1987), 84-85; Dapper (1670), 447; Barbot (1992), 426; Phillips (1746), 226-27; Bosman (1705), 63-64; Van Dantzig (1980), 33, 36, 49.

133 For Cook's Loaf see Pacheco Pereira (1937), 123: Dapper (1670), 447; Barbot (1992), 428 n3; Baesjou (1988), 49 and note 151; a hill 102 meters high, *Africa Pilot* (1967), 458.

134 The terms *Accara/Akra* referred to the nation and territory of what is now called Gã, then bounded by the lagoon near Tema in the east, the Sakumo River in the west, and Akwapim in the north. The city we know as Accra is made up of several towns or villages, each with its own identity: James Town, [*English Accra*], Ussher Town [*Dutch Accra*], Osu [*Danish Accra*], Labade, Teshie, Ningua, Tema. See Reindorf (1895/1966), 11/24; Field (1961), 1-3.

135 For the Accra plains see Boateng (1970), 18-19, 146-48. The "mountains" visible inland are part of the Akuapim-Togo ranges, whose average height in Ghana is 455 meters above sea level.

For the term *Spanish Cavalry* see Robijn/Roggeveen (1971), 24, past Cook's Loaf "you get the highland, called the *Ruiters* or horsemen where you have high Hills within the land."

136 Sokko is commonly known as English Accra or Jamestown. Barbot (1992), 441 n1. For the number of men stationed at James Fort in 1694, see Phillips (1746), 229; in 1697 and 1698 see Davies (1957), 248. See also Bosman (1705), 66-67; Lawrence (1963), 75; Van Dantzig (1980), xii. James Fort is now being used as a prison. For Soco see Baesjou (1988), 20-21. For an illustration and description of James Fort see Barbot (1992), 430-32.

137 Little Accra is also known as Dutch Accra or Usshertown. See Ratelband (1957), lxxv; Bosman (1705), 67; Van Dantzig (1980), xi, 24. The fort, now known as Ussher Fort, was used as a prison until 1993. There are now plans to make it into a museum.

138 This is now Christiansborg Castle and the seat of the government of Ghana, as it was the headquarters for the Danish establishments from 1685 until 1850, when all the Danish possessions in Guinea were sold to the British. Nørregaard (1964), 378ff. See also Barbot (1992), 433, 444 nlo; Bosman (1705), 68; Claridge (1964), 1:172; Reindorf (1980), 3-4.

139 The history of Christiansborg Castle was written, but not published, by Hartvig Meyer, governor from 1703 to 1704. Although not dated, the contents indicate that it had been written shortly after the publication of Tilleman's book in 1697. RA:V-gK 187. Some of the sections could have been either borrowed from Tilleman, or the result of collaboration, since they were colleagues, but additional material and details are included in the Meyer manuscript, and it closes with the installation as governor of Erik Olsen Lugaard by Erick Tilleman on behalf of the Company in 1698. Tilleman has omitted, or did not know, the fact that it was the Swedes who first established a lodge at Osu. The Danes seized the lodge in 1658 from the Swedes as part of Carlofs takeover of the Swedish establishments on behalf of the Danish Glückstadt Company. The lodge came into Dutch hands in 1659, and was reoccupied by the Danes in 1659.

Nørregaard (1966), 42. In 1661 Governor Jost Cramer purchased the site on the beach from King Okai Koi of Accra for "7 marker guld, *eller* 896 Rdr." Meyer (1698?), 1; Wilks (1957), 104; Nørregaard (1966), 42-43. The site on which Christiansborg was built was acquired from Okai Koi in 1650 for 896 riksdalers. Meyer (1698?), 1. For descriptions of the castle see Lawrence (1963), plates 42-50a; for its appearance in the seventeenth century and subsequent aggrandizement, see ibid., 199-205. See also Barbot (1992), plate 41; Bosman (1705), 67-63; Römer (1760), 290-92; Isert (1992), 28-30; Van Dantzig (1980), 30.

140 The king of Accra at that time was Okai Koi. Cf. Wilks (1957), 106-07, 108-09, 111.

141 For Christian Cornelissøn see Nørregaard (1966), 43.

142 There are variations on the identity of Pieter Bolt: a/ Lawrence (1963), 201, writes that "a Greek assistant" instigated the murder of the commander and sold the fort; b/ Nørregaard (1966), 45, writes that the commander, Johan Ulrich, was murdered by the natives, an act instigated by a Greek subordinate. The next commander, Pieter Bold, then sold Christiansborg to the Portuguese; c/ Van Dantzig (1980), 31, writes that the commander was killed by mutineers led by a Greek called Bolten; d/ Meyer (1698?), 1, stated that Christiansborg was traitorously sold to the Portuguese for 36 pounds of gold/9216 riksdalers by "a merchant named Petter Bolth." As in the Tilleman text, the term "Greek" does not appear. However, Barbot reports meeting a Greek there. Perhaps this is the origin of that identity. Barbot (1992), 433, 444n9, 445 nl3. As for the recovery of the castle, Meyer reports that on 24 February 1683 (my emphasis) a message was received at the main Fort Frederiksborg stating that the Portuguese governor, Julius des Champo[*sic*] along with the entire garrison and merchant staff had, under strict orders, left Christiansborg, apart from six men who did not want to leave, and who then went into the Danish service. Meyer (1698?), 2, The Portuguese had renamed the castle *São Francisco Xavier*, and set about making extensive improvements. However, trade did not fulfil expectations, either financially or in

Portuguese relations with the neighboring Africans. After three years or ownership Julião de Campos Barreto (who had been governor of São Tomé earlier), decided that they were ready to leave. They did so in August 1662 and the Akwamu took over immediately, holding the fort until it was returned to the Danes in February 1663. Nørregaard (1966), 46; Vogt (1979), 202-04.

143 In 1689 Nicolaus Janssen Arf (or Arff), was granted by charter exclusive rights to trade in Guinea, rights previously held by the West India and Guinea Company. Similarly, the West Indian trade was granted to Jørgen Thormølen, a merchant from Bergen, Norway. Trade from other countries and from Glückstadt, rivaling Copenhagen, was to be prohibited. However, the capture of the fort, the loss of ships, and dishonesty on the part of assistants conspired to put a halt to Arf's shipping, and he finally gave up his rights to the Guinea trade in 1696. Grove (1904), 234; Nørregaard (1966), 55-62.

144 An Akwamu, *Assameni,* led the seizure and held command throughout the occupation. *King Barsiar* was Bassua, the Akwamuhene, who was acting as regent for the young heir, Prince Ado. Wilks (1957), 120-21. Phillips (1746), 228, describes his experience as a dinner guest of Assemeni, "the Black general" at Christiansborg in May 1694. Bassua was still ruling as "Upper King" or "Old King" when Tilleman, acting as special agent to the Company returned to the Coast, the year after the publication of his book. See Meyer (1698?), 6. The maltreatment of the Danish staff by the Akwamu is described by Meyer thus: they were manhandled, imprisoned, beaten to death; the merchant was barbarously quartered; the governor (Harding Pettersen), was very seriously wounded, having been stabbed in the neck four to five times, his hamstrings nearly severed so he could not run, and then he was thrown into the latrine. However, after nightfall he managed to get out, climb the wall, and make his way, taking two nights, to the Dutch Fort Crèvecoeur a quarter of a mile away. Meyer arrived on the scene just shortly after all this happened. Meyer (1698?), 5. However, his report differs considerably from that given by Phillips, who was also on the scene. Phillips met the "Danes general" [*sic*]—clearly the gov-

ernor, Harding Pettersen—at Cape Coast Castle, where he had taken refuge after leaving Crèvecoeur. According to Phillips, Pettersen "betook him to a window, whence he flung himself out, and fled to the Dutch as before, but not without receiving several wounds, one of which disabled his left arm." Phillips (1746), 228. Phillips provided Pettersen with free passage to Europe, so he had ample opportunity to hear the tale from the victim himself. However, at Principe Pettersen boarded the Danish ship *Christiansborg* which was also carrying Hartvig Meyer. The ships were attacked by the pirate *Long Ben Avery*, and Pettersen was among those who lost their lives. Before that Meyer had also had personal contact with him and must also have had ample opportunity to hear the tale from the victim. Phillips mentions that Pettersen was very reluctant to board the Danish ship for fear of "being harshly treated" because of the loss of the castle to the Akwamu. I venture the suggestion that Pettersen himself embroidered the tale told to Meyer in order to win sympathy and ameliorate his professional predicament. But how could Meyer have missed seeing the "disabled left arm" described by Phillips? See also Barbot (1992), 436-37; Bosman (1705), 67-68; Nørregaard (1966), 58-59.

The castle was recovered in 1694 by Hartvjg Meyer and Johan Thrane, who had left Copenhagen on the ships *Christiansborg* and *Gyldenlöves Vaaben*, knowing nothing of the Akwamu takeover until their arrival on the Coast. After negotiations the castle was returned to the Danes on payment of 3000 riksdalers worth of merchandise. Cf. Meyer (1689?), 5; Wilks (1957), 120-21; Nörregaard (1966), 59. However, the Akwamu retained the keys to the castle, and they are still part of the stool property of Akwamu. Cf. Kyerematen (1964), 47. For other instances of occupation of forts by Africans, see Bosman (1705), 67-68; and Ward (1969), 93 n24.

145 Labat (1730), 311-12: the landing was very difficult and seldom, attempted by sailing vessels or their small boats. They were dependent on the professional canoeists. Barbot (1992), 435, 447-48 nl9; Phillips (1746), 229; Isert (1992), 27-28; Monrad (1822), 350; *Atlantic Ocean Pilot* (1884), 498; Boateng (1970), 4;

Dickson (1971), 115-16; Jones (1985), 189.

146 The wall around Labadi, as described by De Marees (1987), 86, and Dapper (1670), 449, had evidently disappeared by Tilleman's time. See also Barbot (1992), 437, 449 n23; *Africa Pilot* (1967), 461-62. For the Akwamu presence, see Wilks (1957), 112, 119.

147 In declaring the Gold Coast "best," Tilleman was probably thinking of several elements: availability of food and water; a people knowledgeable in trade and communication with Europeans; a coastline permitting the building of forts; the certainty of being able to purchase gold; the availability of slaves, albeit not comparable to the Slave Coast. See Dapper (1670), 448; Barbot (1992), 455; Bosman (1705), 70; Rømer (1760), 127-31.

148 The term "custom" was in general use among the Europeans trading on the coast. Because the Akwamu had subjugated the Gã in 1680, the king would have been the ruler of the Akwamu nation See note 175 below. Barbot (1992), 430; Reindorf (1895), 60-61; Wilks (1957), 106-11. Bosman in *History in Africa* (1976), 93-94, reports the payments as one ounce of gold per month.

149 For the aforementioned forts and "their" towns see Chapter Six, notes 158 and 159. See also Daaku (1970), 155.

150 The Akwamu capital, until 1730, was probably Nyanaoase. Wilks (1957), 106-11; Kea (1982), 34. The former capital of Gã, Great Accra, was about ten miles inland, near Ayawaso. Reindorf (1895/1966), 13/25; Boateng (1970), 150.

151 The king of Accra in 1677 was the already mentioned Okai Koi. For the war against Accra, in which both Okai Koi and his eldest son were killed, see Wilks (1957), 106-07. See also Barbot (1992), 441 n3; Nørregaard (1966), 44-45; Daaku (1970), 154; Kea (1982), 139-40.

152 The Danes supported the Accra in the struggle against the Akwamu, which resulted ultimately in the seizure of Christiansborg in 1693 as an act of revenge. See Daaku (1970), 112, 155. See also Barbot (1992), 431, 436; Bosman (1705), 64-65; Wilks (1957),

108, 120; Kea (1982), 154-55.

153 For the Akwamu King Ansa Sasraku and his campaigns see Wilks (1957), 106ff., 119; Daaku (1970), 154-55.

154 Ado became the new ruler in 1700 after the death of the regent Basua in 1699. Bosman in *History in Africa* (1976), 93-94; Daaku (1970), 113. For a discussion of political differences and division of power between Basua and Ado see Wilks (1957), 120, 122-23.

155 The Akwamu retained control until their defeat by Akim in 1730. Wilks (1957), 112ff., 114-15. For comments on Akwamu oppression and fear of the Akwamu, even in Kormantin, see Phillips (1746), 226. Also Bosman (1705), 64-65.

156 For the Akwamu army see Kea (1982), 138, 161-64.

157 Ibid., 165.

158 Ibid., 123-26, 165.

159 It is likely that a specific, most desirable, part of the animal was designated as tribute to the king. Isert remarks that in Whydah the breast meat of the elephant was always given to the king or viceroy. Isert (1992), 104.

160 In the Akan system the chief held all land himself, Dickson (1969), 76.

161 Kea (1982), 162-63

162 Ibid.

163 Tilleman makes no mention of specialization in these areas. See Bosman (1705), 70-71; Isert (1992), 135, writes of class division of labor.

164 Tilleman's exclusion of metal smiths and hunters may, perhaps, be explained by the fact that these are fairly solitary occupations and their numbers, relative to those involved in fishing, salt-making, etc., would have been small.

165 Boateng (1970), 80, informs us that the best fishing for a

large sea bream is from June to September. De Marees (1987), 123-24, reports that a pike-like fish was caught in great numbers in October-November. I have been unable to identify *pargos*. For sale inland see Isert (1992), 166-67.

166 For the method of salt production from sea water see Isert (1992), 60. Rask (1754), 124-26, writes, "About 40 to 50 Negroes from Akwamu usually come down to Accra nearly every day to buy this salt, often [making] a journey of 8 to 10 miles... where they [the Accras] sell it for slaves and cloth for great profit." See also Barbot (1992), 482-83.

167 Cultivation of crops was carried on in the plains and hills farther inland, where the soil was less sandy, and where quantities of fruit and vegetables could be grown. See Isert (1992), 161, and his attempt at plantation in the hills of Akwapim. Ibid., Appendix 3.

168 Müller writes that in Fetu the richest people had oxen, cows, goats, and sheep brought in, particularly from Accra. This implies a middle step in the coasting/carrying trade, that is, from Allada on the Slave Coast to Accra, thence to Fetu. See Jones (1983), 239. See also De Marees (1987), 130, who mentions sheep brought from São Tomé to the Gold Coast by the Portuguese; Phillips (1746), 237 remarks that cows at Whydah were small and cheap; Bosman (1705), 235.

169 For brokers, see Barbot (1992), 516-18; Kea (1982), 206, 220.

170 For *travat,* see note 44.

171 On the causes of war see Bosman (1705), 178-79; Rask (1754), 152. Fear of the Akwamu also existed farther west in Kormantin. Phillips (1746), 226.

172 The original text of "good manners or [sense of] right" reads *Politie eller Ret.* Tilleman used Roman script for the first word, indicating, as he does in other places, that it is a foreign term. I have interpreted it as indicating the French *politesse. Ret* can mean "right" or "court of law."

173 For a discussion of Akani, its identification and history, see

Van Dantzig (1990), 205-16.

174 For trade routes see Dapper (1670), 460; Phillips (1746), 240; Bosman (1705), 72-74, 77-79; Daaku (1970), 65, 68, 158-59.

175 However, Phillips (1746), 214, remarks that at *Bassam Picolo* [Grand Bassam?] on the Ivory Coast, he bought all the gold "in fatishes," i.e., nuggets.

176 De Marees (1987), 188-90; Müller in Jones (1983), 252-53; Villault (1669), 387-89; Dapper (1670), 460-61; Bosman (1705), 80-81; Römer (1760), 177-79; Isert (1992), 142-43; Garrard (1980), 128ff.; Kea (1982), 204.

177 Dapper (1670), 460; Bosman (1705), 80-81; Rask (1754), 83; Römer (1760), 175; Isert (1992), 143. Tilleman's comment on small kingdoms under Akany jurisdiction confirms Daaku's explanation; cf. note 196.

178 The Akanis were forced to fight the Fetu to retain passage through the Fetu kingdom. See Phillips (1746), 240-41. The identity of Tilleman's "Friderichsberg" might be unclear because of its similarity to the name of the Brandenburg Fort Gross-Friedrichsburg. However, the latter was too far west (at Princes Town), to be included in Tilleman's area of trade, and he had earlier [77] used the same expression of "three main castles" signifying Elmina, Cape Coast, and the Danish Fort Frederiksborg in Fetu. However, at the time of Tilleman's writing in the 1690s, Frederiksborg could no longer be given such status, having been handed over to the British in 1688, and renamed Fort Royal. For a visit to "the *Danes Hill Fort*" and its English factor in 1694 see Phillips (1746), 225.

179 For Akwamu control of routes to the coast see Daaku (1970), 153-55; Garrard (1980), 83; Kea (1982), 249-50, 275.

180 Pure and unadulterated gold was known as "Acany gold." Daaku (1970), 146. Understandably the practice of adulteration of gold was of great concern to the European traders and was generally decried and described in some detail as a *caveat* to their countrymen. It is remarkable that Tilleman, writing a

merchant's guide, omits details of falsification as well as means of testing the gold. See De Marees (1987), 192-95; Brun in Jones (1983), 90; Hemmersam in ibid., 121; Müller in ibid., 250; Barbot (1992), 484-85; Bosman (1705), 81-85; Rask (1754), 79-80; Isert (1992), 86-87; Garrard (1980), 86-89.

181 For the volume of gold exports in the 1680s and 1690s see Garrard (1980), 152-57; Kea (1982), 195. For the use of weights see Garrard (1980), 173 ff.; Kea (1982), 190-91. The Danish *Lod,* used for weighing precious metals and stones, equaled 14.6246 grams; Garrard (1980), 225, tells us that in the mid-seventeenth century the Danes used their own weights based on an ounce of 29.4 grams, thus the *Lod* equaled one-half of that ounce, 14.7 grams. See also Phillips (1746), 222.

Tilleman's comment on the Africans' ability to distinguish troy from *Banco* weights simply by heft is, in my opinion, intended to indicate the Africans' expertise in distinguishing between very similar European weights. Römer informs that "[t]he *Guld-Vægt* which we use on the Coast is called *Troi-Vægt* and is the same as *Cøllnsk-Vægt* [Cologne – weight]; the Danish *Guld-Vægt* (i.e., "bank weight"] against that used on the Coast is as 9 to 8." Römer (1760), 322. But the heavier bank weight could be used to cheat the less experienced traders on Ivory Coast. See Phillips (1746), 214.

182 For the *damma* (*Abrus precatorius*) and *taku* see Garrard (1980), 213, 232-33. For their use in the market see ibid., 173-74; Phillips (1746), 222.

183 *Caparie* is privateering, while *Cofardie* is merchant shipping. For cheating in the use of weights see Müller in Jones (1983), 245, 249-50; Phillips (1746), 214; Rask (1754), 84; Garrard (1980), 173.

184 For proving the purity of gold see Barbot (1992), 485; Isert (1992), 87; Garrard (1980), 182; Jones (1983), 121 nl03. Bosman (1705), 845, writes that the use of *aqua fortis* (nitric acid) was not effective if only a small portion of the mass was an alloy. He preferred winnowing. See also Phillips (1746), 222.

185 For silver used in the adulteration of gold, see Müller in Jones (1983), 250; Barbot (1992), 491 nl4; Rask (1754), 79; Garrard (1980), 87, 88, 109.

186 Cf. Barbot (1992), 778; Phillips (1746), 21-29, 229-30; Isert (1992), 177.

187 Barbot (1992), 775, 781; Phillips (1746), 245; Isert (1992), 181. For millie or Turkish wheat see Jones (1983), 321.

188 One *Potte* = 9.68 liters, two *Potter* = 1 *Kanne*. Isert (1992), 76, 181 suggested smaller rations of not more than three-quarters of a *kanne* daily.

189 Strangely, Tilleman does not mention "horse beans" brought from Europe, as did other writers, such as Barbot (1992), 781; Phillips (1746), 245: Isert (1992), 181. The latter mentions that the slaves like the pearl barley brought from Europe. For foodstuffs purchased in Guinea see Barbot (1992), 790 n30; Römer (1760), 268-69.

190 Slaves not kept in shackles when at sea. Phillips (1746), 245; Barbot (1992), 780; Isert (1992), 177.

191 Barbot (1992), 779. For the brandy allotment of 12 gallons per slave for four months, see Law (1992), 5.

192 Römer (1760), 268-69, advises that the only medication in the ship's chest be anti-scurvy and anti-venereal drugs, but that a few female slaves be provided with malagetta pepper, pimento, palm oil, and limes, from which they can prepare their traditional medicines, which work well for them. He also urges the utmost discretion, even secrecy, in the use of phlebotomy, lest the other slaves misunderstand and think it a method of killing them.

193 *Bossies/boss/booges,* etc., derived from the Portuguese *búzio,* cowry shell, were purchased in East India, the Maldives, and used as currency in West Africa. They were also used in Europe to decorate bridles, and the term *snogepander* [snake skulls], which appears in several Scandinavian sources, arose from the supposition that they looked like/actually were snake skulls. Cf.

Barbot (1992), 641-43; Johnson (1970), 18-21; Jones (1983), 41 n110; Isert (1992), 61 n6.

194 *Conte* derives from the Portuguese *conta*, bead. I have no explanation for *Crebe*, a term also used by the Brandenburgers. Cf. Jones (1985), glossary 313. Perhaps it refers to the *Krepe*, the term used to identify the people living cast of the Volta, the Ewe. Or it could mean the Dutch chevron beads, although they were usually dark blue. See Gordon (1976), 21. Unfortunately Tilleman does not specify in this short list of trade goods which were clearly to be brought from Europe, or whether all of the beads were of European origin, but since he describes *aggrey* beads below as being an article from the Slave Coast which was highly valued on the Gold Coast, the beads here mentioned must have been of European production. For other special beads see De Marees (1987), 53, *contoir teeckens*; Bosman (1705), 119, for *Conte de Terra*. See also Tilleman Chapter Eleven, note 16.

195 For a more detailed list of trade wares see Chapter Eleven. See also De Marees (1987), 51-54; Dapper (1670), 482-83; Barbot (1992), 658: Phillips (1746), 243; Jones (1985), 213-14 n1; Law (1991), 198-206. For changing tastes in wares see Römer (1760), 253; Kea (1982), 207-12, 273ff.

196 The "fortresses" at Whydah at the time of Tilleman's writing would have been the English factory described by Phillips (1746), 231-32, and a Dutch factor-in-residence. See Law (1991), 133. Both French and Portuguese factories were reported in 1681-82. Ibid, 135. On the Slave Coast there was a strict system of control both at Allada and Whydah, where trade was conducted by a special officer, "Captain"/*Yevogan*, who was immediately responsible to the king. There were also special interpreters for each nation. Law (1991), 206-08. See also Dapper (1670), 483; Barbot (1992), 620, 637; Bosman (1705), 361a-362a. The same system was still in force one hundred years later. Cf. Isert (1992), 97-98.

197 Uncharacteristically, Tilleman reverses the geographical order of appearance of the three places mentioned here. The

course was always eastward, but Popo is west of Allada and Whydah, and would have been encountered first. Possibly he is here listing them in order of importance to the trade—at the end of the seventeenth century the slave trade at Popo was in decline. Bosman (1705), 334 describes a Danish ship in 1698 which acquired 500 slaves at Popo in twice the time it took Bosman to purchase 2000 at Whydah. For the lodges see Barbot (1992), 635-36. Lawrence (1963), 42, 51. For the history and development of lodges see Barbot (1992), 620-21, 635-37; Law (1991) for Allada 118-27, Whydah 127-41, Popo 141-48.

198 In 1694 the *Hannibal* took on its full complement of 700 and the *East India Merchant* look on 650. Phillips (1746), 230. For the volume of slave exports from the Slave Coast from the 1680s to late 1690s see Law (1991), 158-64. See also Kea (1982), 222-23.

199 See *Africa Pilot* (1967), 477, for the heavy surf off Ouidah Plage. For a description of the transfer of wares from ship to boat to canoe, see Phillips (1746), 221. He also reports that the slaves were sent to the ship when 50 or 60 had been purchased. Ibid., 234, See also Bosman (1705), 337; Jones (1985), 189; Law (1991), 117-18.

200 Dapper(1670), 480-81; Barbot (1992), 339-40, 389-92, 634; Phillips (1746), 230; Bosman (1705), 342, 392; Oettinger in Jones (1985), 192; Law (1990), 31-41. 44-45.

201 The "true" aggrey bead appears to have been a light blue, translucent bead. De Marees (1987), 225 n6; Brun in Jones (1983), 69; Müller in ibid., 204; Barbot (1992), 657; Bosman (1705), 113; Rask (1754), 136; Isert (1992), 114, writes of aggrey beads, describing them as mosaic (he may have been referring to the imported Venetian *millefiore* beads), but verifying the high value placed on them; Fage (1962), 345; Fage (1980), 209; Eriksen (1969), 51; Gordon (1976), 15; Kalous (1979). 211, 213, 217; DeCorse (1989), 44; Law (1991), 46, 192-93.

202 Cowries [*Cypraea moneta*] were strung in units of 40 and the system operated in larger units *of 200* and 4000, Law (1991),

49-50. For an indication of the quantities of cowries necessary, see the trade lists in Law (1992), 3, 7, 8, *et passim*. See also Phillips (1746), 243; *supra*, note 215; Johnson (1970), 18, 35, 42-43.

203 Tilleman is probably referring to the war of 1692-1693 when Ofori (the former king of Accra who had settled with his followers near Little Popo), attacked Whydah, destroying the coastal town of Offra. Law (1991), 245-47. Also Phillips (1746), 236. Regarding the use of firearms, the end of the seventeenth century was in fact a period of transition, and the use of firearms was being more widely adopted. Kea (1971), 194-99; Law (1991), 100-01, 227-28. See also Barbot (1992), 641; Bosman (1705), 394-96.

204 For the acquisition of slaves, see Römer (1760), 125-27, 145, 207-08; Law (1990, 184-85, 187-90, 223, 226. Tilleman's indignation in the final sentence is not fully justified. His contemporary, Philiips, admitted that when an African merchant failed to make good a debt to the Europeans, the latter *panyarred* (seized) inhabitants of the debtor's town to the (slave), value of the debt, thus forcing the debtor's family or friends to make good the debt for the release of those *panyarred*, or they would be sold as slaves. Phillips (1746), 222. For *panyarring* see Isert (1992), 134 n48.

205 Since the early writers frequently generalized from specific phenomena, attributing the practices or beliefs of one group to an entire region, indeed to all of Africa, it is often difficult for the modern reader to pinpoint the locus of practice and practitioners. Tilleman appears here to have finished with the Slave Coast and is back on the Gold Coast, without specifying the switch. However, since "comfu" is an Akan term, and the Gã used many loanwords from Akan, it is safe to assume that the following material is relevant to the Gã area. Christaller defines *okòmfó* as a "fetish-man" possessed with, or prophesying by, a fetish; "the komfo pretends to be the interpreter and mouthpiece either of the guardian spirit of a nation, town or family." The Gã have no "fetish" in the sense of an inanimate object which houses a spirit. Their priests are *wulomo*. Field (1961), 4.

The *akomfo,* or *wóyei,* are, in effect, mediums; and are supported materially by the worshippers. Ibid., 8, 100 *et passim.*

206 For practice of fetish priests, see Hemmersam in Jones (1983), 19; Müller in ibid., 162, 164-65; Bosman (1705), 151-53, 154; Römer (1760), 70-71.

207 For the sabbath and "good days" and "bad days", see De Marees (1987), 67; Müller in Jones (1983), 231; Bosman (1705), 160; Rask (1754), 17, 168; Römer (1760), 85-86; Dickson (1969), 77-78.

208 Barbot (1992), 579-80; Bosman (1705), 147-54; Römer (1760), 51-52, 58, 63, 68ff.; Isert (1992), 128-29, 162; Field (1961), for the *Woyei* (mediums) and their activities, see 100-09, 110ff. For a discussion of "belief" and "religious" participation see Brenner (1989), 87-103.

209 Again Tilleman has succumbed to temptation and has made three sweeping statements which are not tenable. First, to the best of my knowledge, *all* Gã children were not circumcised, but boys were and here Tilleman has got it right—at about the age of eight. Admittedly, De Marees (1987), 23, states that both boys and girls were circumcised and that this was a festive occasion. I feel sure that he had confused the name day or "outdooring" ceremony for one of circumcision, because "outdooring" was/is cause for celebration but there was/is no special ceremony connected with circumcision. Bosman (1705), 210, speaks of "the children" in this respect, a remark I take to be simply a case of carelessness. But Römer, who undoubtedly enjoyed a much closer, and highly personal, relationship with the Gã, specifically limits the practice to the male children. Römer (1760), 88-89. The same information is stated unequivocally in Isert (1992), 131. Modern sources make this distinction as well. See Field (1961), 176; Kilson (1974), 49. Second, (given unclear apposition in the same sentence), if Tilleman is claiming that the Jews circumcised their male children at the age of seven or more, he is mistaken. It occurs on the eighth day of the boy's life. *Genesis* 17:12. Third, this "is not done anywhere else on the entire Coast" is, of course, decidedly not the case.

The Akan did not follow the practice, but other peoples on the Coast did. For the Mende of Sierra Leone, see Little (1951), 115, 119; for Dahomey see Herskovits, (1938), 1:195-99; for the Ewe, see Spieth (1906), 226-27; for the Adangme, see Huber (1963), 19, 24, 94, 154.

210 *Millie/milhio/milho*, the Akan term *awua/awio*, and Turkish wheat indicate maize. For Zea mays see Abbiw (1990), 23-24. For a discussion on the introduction of maize to West Africa from the West Indies see Alpern (1992), 24-45. See also De Marees (1987), 110-11, 113-14; Dapper (1670), 457; Müller in Jones (1983), 205, Appendix A. 425; Bosman (1705), 296-97; Dickson (1969), 78-79.

211 For millet see Dapper (1670), 457; Bosman (1705), 220-22, 297-98; Jones (1983), Appendix A, 426. For *Pennisetum americanum* see Abbiw (1990), 25; Dickson (1969), 79.

212 *Aduba* is a general term for beans. D.K. Abbiw (personal communication); Müller in Jones (1983), 228; ibid., Appendix A. 421; Bosman (1705), 300. See also Abbiw (1990), 32-33 for edible beans.

213 For the term *pegla*, see note 40. For *Oryza sativa* see Abbiw (1990), 24. Müller makes no mention of it. For rice in Cape Verde area, see Barbot (1992), 73, around Axim, 341, along the Coast, 455. It was not common all along the Coast, but was grown only at Axim and Ante, where it was of a poor quality. Bosman (1705), 298; Dickson (1969), 79. In modern times it is grown in the forest zone of Ghana and in the northern savanna. Boateng (1970), 68, 74. See also Alpern (1992), 20-01.

214 By "travat season" Tilleman means the principal rainy season. Dapper (1760), 471; Ulsheimer in Jones (1983), 30; Müller in ibid, 220; Boateng (1970), 67-68.

215 Müller in Jones (1983), 230; ibid., Appendix A. 438; Bosman (1705), 289-90, For lime juice as a preventative against scurvy, a practice already established in the seventeenth century, see Barbot (1992), 461. Abbiw (1990), 43, lists seven varieties now being cultivated.

216 For Sour or Seville Oranges, *C. aurantium*, see Abbiw (1990), 43. Also Dapper (1670), 457; Barbot (1992), 461; both sweet and bitter varieties at Axim, Bosman (1705), 239.

217 Tilleman's term is clearly a derivation or corruption of the Akan term *abwérew*. There are two varieties in Ghana today: one, the white variety, is used as chewing cane; the other, red, is used for the extraction of juice for sugar. Abbiw (1990), 74. See also Jones (1983), Appendix A. 436; see also De Marees (1987), 63, 158-59; Müller in Jones (1983), 227-28; Barbot (1992), 461.

218 *Patattas/batattas* are sweet potatoes. For *Ipomoea batatas* see Abbiw (1990), 29. De Marees (1987), 164, 166: Müller in Jones (1983), 227; Bosman (1705), 299; Alpern (1992), 26.

219 For yams see De Marees (1987), 163-64, drawing 166; Barbot (1992), 460; Bosman (1705), 299; Dickson (1969), 79; Abbiw (1990), 27-28.

220 Tilleman's terms *bannanas*, or *broddi*, refer to plantains *Musa paradisiaca*. *Baccoves* are bananas *M. paradisiaca var. sapientum*. Abbiw (1990), 30, 44. Müller in Jones, 225-26; Barbot (1992), 466 n5; Bosman (1705), 291; Alpern (1992), 19-20.

221 This is pineapple, whose pungent flavor was frequently described as "hot" or "warm." Dapper (1670), 457; De Marees (1987), 163; Müller in Jones (1983), 230-31; Bosman (1705), 301-04, did not like its acidity; on the other hand, Isert (1992), 142, was very much taken by the plant, not only for its refreshing flavor but for the utility of its fibers. Alpern (1992), 29. Tilleman was apparently correct in his final statement. See Abbiw (1990), 44 for *Ananas comosus*, "Wild varieties grow in the forest although the crop is basically a savanna one... It is now half-naturalized in tropical Africa."

222 Müller in Jones (1983), 231. For wild fruits see Abbiw (1990), 46-49.

223 *Turreba* is probably derived from the Akan *nto rowa*, aubergine. Müller in Jones (1983), 228; Abbiw (1990), 38, Egg plants *Solanum*. See also Alpern (1992), 17.

224 *Apperaba* is probably a version of the Akan term *aparre-besja*. For Pepper, *Capsicum annum*, see Abbiw (1990), 35. See Jones (1983), Appendix A. 428. Tilleman made the same comparison as Müller, who described the peppers as looking like "elongated raisins." Müller in Jones (1983), 229. See also Hemmersam in Jones (1983), 112; Bosman (1705), 305.

225 This is the kola nut, which is indigenous in the forest area and has been an important export article since prehistoric times, both to the northern savanna and to the coastal areas, although the latter trade has decreased in recent years. Boateng (1970), 87; Abbiw (1990), 72-73, *Cola nitida*. The kola nut contains caffeine, and has an astringent effect on the mouth. Müller in Jones (1983), 229-30; Bosman (1705), 307, 307n.

226 Clearly, this is pawpaw/papaya, *Carica papaya*. I am unable to explain the term *Spansk Spek*. The fruit is used as a fruit when ripe, as vegetable when immature, and the root is used as a salt substitute. Abbiw (1990), 45. It was not mentioned by De Marees or Müller. Barbot did not mention it in the 1688 edition but it was included in the 1732 edition. Barbot (1992), 466 n8. See also Bosman (1705), 290-91; Rask (1754), 98-99; Alpern (1992), 29.

227 For coconuts, *Cocos nucifera*, see Hemmersam in Jones (1983), 124; Barbot (1992), 462-63; Bosman (1705), 288-89; Abbiw (1990), 67-68. Müller made no mention of this tree.

228 The Oil Palm, *Elaeis guineensis*, is indigenous to tropical Africa. Abbiw (1990), 68-69. See Lübelfing in Jones (1983), 16; Brun in ibid., 52; Müller in ibid., 223-24; Barbot (1992), 461; Bosman (1705), 285-86; Rask (1754), 47-48, 99-100.

229 Horses were few in number on the Gold Coast because they commonly became infected by the bite of the tsetse fly. Those that were there were evidently small and weak. Several authors said there were none. De Marees (1987), 129; Barbot (1992), 469; Bosman (1705), 238; Rask (1754), 103. Horses on the Slave Coast (whence Tilleman says they were brought to the Gold Coast), were probably imported from the interior from

the Yoruba. Law (1991), 36-37. All of the early sources write that cows were not milked, apart from one source which mentions butter made at Cape Verde. Ulsheimer in Jones (1983), 29. See also De Marees (1987), 129; Dapper (1670), 458; Bosman (1705), 236, who remarks that where they were milked, at Elmina, the results were exceedingly poor; Rask (1754), 95, 102-03; Dickson (1969), 81-82.

230 Tilleman's comment on domestic birds is not quite clear as to provenance. His claim is that those brought "by the Christians" do not thrive, so he may have meant birds brought from Europe. Other authors report that the Portuguese brought domestic birds from São Tomé and that they thrived. De Marees (1987), 130; Dapper (1670), 458; Bosman (1705), 240. For sheep, goats, and pigs see De Marees (1987), 130; Dapper (1670), 458; Bosman (1705), 236-37; Dickson (1969), 82.

231 Tilleman's listing of animals indicates a lack of personal knowledge, indeed a lack of interest. Presumably Tilleman's time and interest were concentrated on trade, on shuttling between the road and the castle and its immediate surrounds, but it was expected that an account dealing with Africa must include something about animals. His experience of animals would have been limited to the area around Accra, to game brought for sale at the markets, or to hearsay. The result is that his catalog has so few details that true identification is impossible. I have been fortunate in having Alan Tye available as a consultant, and all the information he provided and the comments he made on birds, animals, and reptiles will be recorded in the footnotes as "(p.c)."

232 The elephants are *Loxodonta africana* ; the lions *Panthera leo;* the buffaloes *Syncerus caffer*. Eland (*Tragelaphus derbianus*), no longer occurs in Ghana, nor is there any proof that it ever did. Tilleman may have meant some other large antelopes such as Waterbuck (*Kobus ellipsiprymnus*), Kob (*Kobus kob*), Roan (*Hippotragus equinus*), or Hartebeest (*Alcelaphus buselaphus*), which, although not present there now may have been found there in Tilleman's day. The same applies to "hart" and "three

varieties of deer." To the latter one might add gazelles and duiker, *Steen-Bukke*, later described as resembling a European roe deer, probably indicated duikers *Cephalophus* spp. (small antelopes), or Bushbuck *Tragelaphus scriptus*. "Tiger" was probably leopard (*Panthera pardus*), and "leopards" may have been smaller spotted cats (e.g., *Profelis aurata*), but it is impossible to make an identification without more details. By "wolves" Tilleman meant some kind of wild canid or hyaena. Civet cats, mentioned by all the other authors, are the African Civet *Viverra civetta*. By "large porcupines" he probably meant Crested Porcupine *Hystrix cristata*. Hares must have been Whyte's Hare *Lepus whytei*. The listing of "forest cat" is again too vague for identification. Tilleman may also have included catlike animals, such as the genet in this group. Alan Tye (p.c.).

I have attempted to identify the vernacular terms listed by Tilleman, and have found, in Christaller, *kokobo*, a small beast of prey the size of a small cat, ?a weasel; *adòmpó*, a wild dog, bush dog. *Agviri* might be *Agwirri*, Jones (1983), Appendix A. no. 172, where it is identified as a species of squirrel. So much for Tilleman's "forest cats." But he was correct in listing *Abakaw*, Fante *abaku*, Golden cat *Projelis aurata*. Adam Jones (p.c.). The small apes would have been any of a considerable variety of monkeys, and the large apes would undoubtedly have been Chimpanzee *Pan troglodytes* and Baboon *Papio cynocephalus*. Alan Tye (p.c.)

For other early references to animals, see De Marees (1987), 130-32; Müller in Jones (1983), 240-43; Villault (1669), 373; Dapper (1670), 458; Barbot (1992), 469; Bosman (1705), 241-46, 247-56; Rask (1754), 103-11.

233 The catalog of bird names is equally frustrating for its lack of identifying characteristics. The species are too numerous to permit a guess. The only clues to identification are: wild geese, which can only be the Spur-winged Goose, *Plectropterus gambensis*; and "blue parrots," a term also used by the Dutch, to indicate the Grey Parrot, *Psittacus erithacus*. The crow would have been the Pied Crow, *Corvus albus*, and tame pigeons, *Columba livia*, which were brought from Europe. Alan Tye (p.

c.). For other early references to birds, see De Marees (1987), 133-35; Villault (1669), 374-76; Dapper (1670), 458-59; Bosman (1705), 262-71; Rask (1754), 112-16.

234 Understandably Tilleman was much more familiar with many varieties of fish, most of which were also described and identified by Müller in his vocabulary. Tilleman has painstakingly followed Müller's order of listing (with some variation in orthography), thus saving himself the trouble of selection and arrangement. However, the descriptions are his own. See Jones (1983), Appendix A. numbers 212-33. De Marees (1987), 125, explains his avoidance of vernacular names because he could get no uniform information on them, and thus found it improper to try to reproduce them.

235 Burrito. See Müller in Jones (1983), 233: Bosman (1705), 278-79 for *aboie*; Rask (1754), 19 for *aboes*.

236 Red Mullet or Sea Bream. Müller in Jones (1983), 233; Bosman (1705), 278. This is probably the fish called *sinkesu* by several of the Danish writers, Rask (1754), 7, 19: Isert (1992), 126.

237 Sardine. De Marees (1987), 120; Müller in Jones (1983), 234; Villault (1669), 377; Bosman (1705), 279; Rask (1754), 19; Isert (1992), 126.

238 Flying Fish. De Marees (1987), 122; Müller in Jones (1983), 234; Villault (1669), 377-78; Barbot (1992), 526.

239 Spanish Mackerel or Kingfish. De Marees (1987), 123; Müller in Jones (1983), 234; Bosman (1705), 278.

240 Threadfin. Hemmersam in Jones (1983), 114; Müller in ibid, 235; Bosman (1705), 278 "flat noses."

241 Sting Ray. Müller in Jones (1983), 235; Bosman (1705), 279.

242 Dolphin Fish. The name implies a golden color. De Marees (1987), 154; Müller in Jones (1983), 235: Rask (1754), 20-21

243 For *Ekam Samman* see Müller in Jones (1983), 235. Jones notes that there is an orthographical error, that *ekam* should be *ennam*. That Tilleman should make the same error testifies

to his careful copying of Müller's list, albeit giving his own descriptions in most cases. Christaller has *enām nsunām*, fish (*enām* meaning the flesh or meat of any animal). The term *osāmān*, means ghost, specter, according to Christaller. It is difficult to know which of the two terms Müller, and Tilleman, intended when they called it "devil fish."

244 Shark. De Marees (1987), 124, 156; Müller in Jones (1983), 236; Villault (1669), 378; Barbot (1992), 520-21, 523-24; Rask (1754), 17.

245 Sea Pike, De Marees (1987), 124; Müller in Jones (1983), 236; Bosman (1705), 278.

246 ?Corcovado, from the Portuguese "curved." Müller in Jones (1983), 236, 236 n432; Rask (1754), 19, of which one provides a full meal for three men.

247 Guitar Fish. Müller in Jones (1983), 237; Rask (1754), 25. The latter identifies this fish as *Pisce di Diabolo*, and one wonders about Tilleman's *Pisse Diable* as a name for the fish no. 9 above. There appears to be either a confusion of terms, or the name was used ubiquitously.

248 Tilleman's reference must be to no. 2 *Wiwrye* above. Müller in Jones (1983), 237; Bosman (1705), 278. *Pargos* may be *Sparus pargrus*. Chris Gordon (p.c.).

249 Ibacore, a large pelagic tuna. De Marees (1987), 155, 155 n4; Rask (1754), 20, the meat of the head and belly taste best, the rest is tasteless.

250 For Bonito and Albacore see De Marees (1987), 154-55; Müller in Jones (1983), 238. All three fish are species of tuna.

251 Lobster. For lobster and langouste see Rask (1754), 21. Also De Marees (1987), 123. The local name is *po-sesew* for a *Panulirus* sp. Chris Gordon (p.c.).

252 Müller in Jones (1983), 238-39; Barbot (1992), 521. Rask (1754), 21, claims that they are especially large when harvested at full moon. Isert (1992), 75, 81, says that those that grow in the

branches of the mangrove trees at the Volta River have the best flavor when the river is salty. The large ones are *O. denticulata*, and the small variety are *O. tulipa*. Gordon (p c.).

253 Müller in Jones (1983), 239.

254 Jones (1983), Appendix A. no. 229, Grey Mullet. Also Bosman (1705), 279; Rask (1754), 20; Isert (1992), 33-34.

255 For *Patavia* see Müller in Jones (1983), 239; Bosman (1705), 279.

256 For fishing methods see De Marees (1987), 120ff.; Müller in Jones (1983), 231-333 *passim*; Barbot (1992), 519-21; Bosman (1705), 129-30; Rask (1754), 21-24; Isert (1992), 142; Monrad (1822), 138-40, includes a method of drugging fish by sprinkling certain herbs on the water; Dickson (1969), 83-84.

257 For "fetish fish" see Barbot (1992), 521.

258 Tilleman's final statement is unclear. By "in the countries here" he may mean either Europe or the Guinea Coast. The snake described is the Rock Python, *Python sebae*, the only African snake this big, but there are far more than four other species in Ghana. Alan Tye (p.c,). See De Marees (1987), 128; Hemmersam in Jones (1983), 126-27; Müller in Jones (1983), 161, worshipped at Frederiksborg; Barbot (1992), 649 n13; Isert (1992), 105, 106-07, 128.

259 Tilleman's term probably derives from the Dutch *leguaan*, and actually refers to the iguana. What he means is the Nile Monitor, *Varanus niloticus*, which does make good eating and is found near rivers. Alan Tye (p.c.), See also De Marees (1987), 128, 146-47.

260 Tilleman is probably referring to the Rainbow Lizard *Agama agama*. Alan Tye (p.c,). But it is remarkable that he neglected to mention the colors. See Rask (1754), 243 for *hagadis*.

261 In fact the small scorpions are more venomous than the large ones. Alan Tye (p.c.). Barbot (1992), 278; Bosman (1705), 275; Rask (1754), 244-45.

262 Tilleman seems to have confused the millipede, which does not sting, with the centipede, which is nocturnal and does bite. *Tusind-been* means millipede and it does resemble the "cabbage worm," the caterpillar of the Cabbage White butterfly. Preben Enhard (p.c.),

263 *Kaymanos* probably refers to the Long-snouted Crocodile, *Crocodylus cataphractus*, The large ones are the Nile Crocodile *C. niloticus*. Alan Tye (p.c.). See De Marees (1987), 146; Hemmersam in Jones (1983), 125; Rask (1754), 123, 162, 243; Isert (1992), 80.

264 Tilleman's list of trade articles, as are most of the others in contemporary sources, is fairly general, and the contents are similar. See Dapper (1670), 473-74.For details of these articles, their purchase and sale prices in mid-century see Ratelband (1953), xcii-cx. For examples of actual quantities and value in the purchase of slaves in the 1680s and 1690s see Nörregaard (1951), 61-65; Law (1992), 3; Jones (1985), 18 n1. Barbot (1992), 562 n4, remarks that the Danes and the Brandenburgers purchased their cargo in Holland "commonly consisting of very near the same sort of wares...the two former having hardly any thing of their own, proper for the trade of the Gold Coast." For several items Tilleman suggests a number of varieties [*slags*] where he probably meant sizes [*störrelser*].

265 Iron was a necessary import and takes pride of place in the list of trade articles. This was not due to the Africans being unable to produce their own iron but may have attested to a lack of ability to produce enough for their needs. Perhaps lack of sufficient fuel was a contributory factor. See Hair (1989), 13-14; Thornton (1992), 45-46. The requirement that they be "stamped"-presumably with the mark of the manufacturer-is curious, and one that is lacking in other lists. However, "voyage iron" found in the wreck of the *Henriette Marie*, which sank off the coast of Florida in 1700, did have stamps on it. (Christopher De Corse, personal communication). One might speculate on Tilleman's insistence-perhaps it was to insure that it was iron from Scandinavia and not, for example, from England that

was being shipped. De Marees (1987), 52, 56, tells how the bars were measured. Ratelband (1953), cix , lists bars weighing 30-31 pounds as an extremely important trade item. When the *Charlotta Amalia* sailed from Copenhagen in 1674 she had 2,000 iron bars in her hold. Nørregård (1951), 62. In 1681, at Allada, iron bars were in little demand, but in 1686 they were again a desirable article of trade. See Law (1990a), 27; idem (1991), 200-01; idem (1992), Documents 41, 43, 44. See also Barbot (1992), 562 n3; Jones (1985), 25, 55; Thornton (1992), 46-48.

266 Copper articles such as pans and bracelets appear on most lists, but in the form of rods I have found them less frequently listed. See Müller in Jones (1983) 247. Ratelband (1953), cii-iii, and Jones (1985), 132, 137.

267 Cauldrons of this particular description do not appear in other lists, to the best of my knowledge. Tilleman may have been referring to "band-kettles" whose rolled rim was reinforced with a strip of iron. Jones (1985), 312.

268 *Vielse* is probably an early form of *vidde* width, diameter in this context. These very large pans were probably the "big Scottish Pans, not less than 2 fathoms in circumference" [3-8 feet in diameter] used for slaughtering goats and pigs. De Marees (1987), 51-52. Ratelband (1953), cvii-cviii, speaks of copper basins of a diameter of "1 el and more." For testing the strength of the pan see De Marees (1987), 56. On other lists the weight rather than the size is stated. Jones (1985), 136, 139, *et passim*.

269 These were known as manillas and were also used as currency. De Marees (1987), 52-53; Ratelband (1953), xcvii-viii; Hair (1989), 15; Law (1992), 3, 11.

270 An interesting insight into the vagaries of the trade comes from the recovery of the cargo of the English slave ship Henrietta Marie (see n. 2). There was an impressive amount of pewterware, as well as green and yellow beads. Since the ship was on her homeward voyage there can be no doubt that these articles, loaded in England for anticipated trade in Africa, had not been saleable after all. Moore (1989) 199, 201. For *manggods*,

see Glossary. De Marees (1987), 52, 53.

271 Ibid., 54.

272 Ibid., 53.

273 Tilleman uses the term *slags* types, but he probably meant *störrelser* sizes. See Ratelband (1953), cix, for three sizes.

274 This article was not commonly listed, but see Brun in Jones (1983), 55.

275 A fusil is a light flintlock firearm; a carbine is a short-barreled lightweight firearm; a musket is a long caliber shoulder firearm. For the traffic in firearms in the late seventeenth century see Kea (1971), 192-96. Also Nørregárd (1951), 61-62. Muskets, carbines, and occasionally long guns appear on all the lists of trade goods brought by the Brandenburgers. Jones (1985), 60-74. For the trade on the Slave Coast see Law (1991), 202-03.

276 *Slange-Krud* meant coarse gunpowder suitable for small cannons.

277 De Marees (1987) 52; Ratelband (1953), c, cii.

278 *Fyrstaal* refers specifically to steel used with flint to start a fire, I have only found steel mentioned in one other place. See Jones (1985), 115. See Thornton (1992), 46, for early production of steel in Africa.

279 For *bossies* or snake skulls see note 215. For the importance of cowries and the amounts necessary see Law (1990a), Letter 7; idem (1992), 48-50. See also Johnson (1970), 34-35, 37, 42-43, 332.

280 See Chapter Nine n9. Beads have been an important item of trade for centuries. See DeCorse (1989), 41, 43-44. They appeared on all the European trade lists, often as "corals", and generally with a number of specific names. See Jones (1985), Appendix C: *conte carbe*, lavender, *lemoen,* madrigette, olivette, *orange pars(t)*, pipe beads, *quispel, rosados,* a list which, conveniently for our Tilleman list, totals nine. This does not imply plagiarism because Jones has culled the name from all the Brandenburg documents (which I assume Tilleman did not pe-

ruse) so presumably they were the most common. De Marees (1987), 53, 56, relates that the prospective buyer counted every bead on each string. See also Ratelband (1953), ciii-vii; Erikson (1969), 51, 57, 59, 62 photograph; Gordon and Kahan (1976),5-7, 19-21 for Venetian and Dutch beads.

281 Clearly this indicates true coral. See Müller in Jones (1983), 247; Isert (1992), 109.

282 Ratelband (1953), cviii.

283 Tobacco was grown in West Africa but the Africans preferred the Brazilian variety. Isert (1992), 139. See also Law (1991), 203-04.

284 The Dutch sent tallow in larger containers weighing 25 pounds. Ratelband (1953), cviii.

285 *Flaske-fodere* are cases provided with divisions for the transport of bottles. Thus, the brandies in this item would be bottled rather than in ankers.

286 An *anker* held 38-39 liters. For an example of quantities and types of containers, see Jones (1985), 129-30 and Appendix C; Ratelband (1953), xcix. Brandy was in constant demand for several purposes: as a trade article; as provision for ships' crews and slaves during sea journeys; for the Europeans' consumption, and private trade, at the factories and castles; as a gift to prominent people; for pouring libations on religious and official occasions and to seal agreements; and as acknowledgement for services rendered, known then, and today, as "dash." See Jones (1985), 135 n.1.

287 By "well-packed" Tilleman is probably advising that care be taken to prevent the growth of mould on the cloth during the long sea voyage, that is, that it not only be clean but perfectly dry before being packed tightly into the chests. See also Ratelband (1953), cviii, for *Slaaplakens*.

288 De Marees (1987), 51, 55-56; Law (1991), 201-02.

289 *Fufu* means white. Jones (1983), Appendix A. no. 269.

290 For Indian textiles see Glossary. Also Jones (1983), Appendix A. nos. 256 ff. For the cloth trade from India to England to Guinea in mid-seventeenth century, see Makepeace (1989), 239-41.

291 *Say* is a finely woven woolen cloth resembling serge. Ratelband (1953), cvii; Jones (1985), Appendix C; Law (1992), Appendix I.

292 *Perpetuana* is a high quality woolen cloth. Ratelband (1953), cvii, remarks that it was cut into bias strips and used as girdles/sashes. Phillips (1746), 236, tells us that *perpetuans* and *says*, especially the blue ones, were unraveled and rewoven to make "Whidaw or Allada cloths" of blue and white stripes, and that these were sold to the Europeans for further sale in Barbados.

293 *Grosgrøn* is probably grogram, a loosely woven fabric of silk and mohair or wool, often stiffened with gum.

294 One *alen* = 68.81 cm. Ribbons are also mentioned by Müller in Jones (1983), 247. For a discussion of the cloth trade both as an import article from Europe and an export article via the Europeans to other African countries and even the West Indies, see Daaku (1970), 34-40; Thornton (1992), 48-53.

295 Barbot (1992) 559, mentions black hats. European hats were frequently used in combination with traditional dress. See Müller in Jones (1983), 205; Isert (1992), 94.

296 This awkward statement seems to be testifying to the low value of the small articles mentioned, i.e. there is so little demand for them in the slave/gold trade that they are only useful for private trade in the local markets.

297 Tilleman is referring here to the entire Guinea coast because the articles mentioned were procured from trading from Cape Verde to São Thomé.

298 Barbot (1992), 485, 492 n16; Phillips (1746), 222. Bosman (1705), 89-91, noted that amounts varied in times of war and peace. There was a drop in exports from 1698 to 1704 during the Asante-Denkyira wars. Daaku (1970), 27. Rask (1754), 79,

stated that the decline in gold purchases was due to the interlopers. For gold exports from mid-seventeenth century to the beginning of the eighteenth century, see Bean (1974) 352-53. For the amounts exported from 1601 and dwindling by 1701, see Garrard (1980), 152-57. See also Jones (1985), 6, 10; Fair (1989), 15-16.

299 Marees (1987) 12; Ulsheimer in Jones (1983) 29 and n35.

300 Civet was evidently taken on both as the extract, in jars, and by the purchase of civet cats. De Marees (1987), 131; Phillips (1746), 229; Law (1991), 197.

301 Cf. Dapper (1670), 429; Rask (1754), 29, especially at River Sess; Jones (1985), 56, 185; Law (1991), 192. For classifying tusks by weight see Isert (1992), 85-86.

302 Earlier in the book ([21]) Tilleman claimed that the best rice on the entire coast was at Cape Mesurado. Hemmersam in Jones (1983), 101, purchased rice in Sierra Leone. Bosman (1705), 431, bought great quantities at the River Sess. The Brandenburgers bought it at Cape Verde and the River Sess. Jones (1985), 24, 34.

303 *Greyn*/maiagette was purchased largely on the Grain Coast. See Tilleman [25] for the Portuguese from São Thomé buying it in great quantities. True pepper was grown and purchased in Benin. Ulsheimer in Jones (1983), 24-25.

304 For *Bukke/Stenbukke* see note 256. For hides see Dapper (1670), 430; Barbot (1992), 153.

305 This undoubtedly means dye wood/camwood/logwood/campeachy, various varieties of wood used for both dyeing and coloring. This was also an important article in the West Indian trade. De Marees (1987), 233 n29; Barbot (1992), 718, 720 n4; Isert (1992), 199; Jones (1983), 26 n28, 47 n13.

306 Mats were a considerable article of trade to England. Thornton (1992), 53.

307 Tilleman evidently means that all of the wares listed from

1-12 were taken back to Europe. Phillips (1746), 249, states that the local sugar was coarse and dirty but that the sugar that had been brought to São Thomé from Brazil was good. See also Hemmersam in Jones (1983), 133; Müller (ibid.), 227; Jones (1985), 56.

308 For Aggrey beads see n200. For the carrying/coastal/cabotage trade see note 333.

309 The European ships did not limit their activity to trading European goods for African gold, ivory and slaves. They also carried African goods from one country to another, particularly cloth from Allada and beads from Benin back to the Gold Coast. Slaves were sold at São Thomé. Zur Eich in Jones (1983), 267-68; Jones (1985), 19; Law (1989), 229-33. See also De Marees (1987), 225 n6; Dapper (1670), 429-30; Daaku (1970), 24-45; Kea (1991), 208, 216-23; *idem* (1982), 216, 219; Law (1991), 192-94, 195; Thornton (1992), 50-52.

310 For knick-knacks see De Marees (1987), 53-54.

311 These were the three ships which Nikolai Jensen Arf sent out as soon as he was granted exclusive trading rights in Guinea. Nörregaard (1966), 55-56.

312 See *Africa Pilot* (1967), 54, for changing wind directions north of Cape Verde. Rainy seasons, generally, with high humidity...considerable rainfall...little air movement "tend to have an adverse effect on ships and equipment generally, as well as on personnel, and have earned for some of these tropical coasts the reputation of being the 'white man's grave.'" Since this was written in 1967 for motor-driven ships, Tilleman's *caveat* would have been even more important for sailing ships. Barbot (1992), 225 n1.

313 Phillips (1746), 229 remarks that the anchor must be weighed "every night and morning, lest it should settle so far into the clay as not to be able to get it up. Few ships come here but leave their anchors behind them..."

314 For *travat/travado* see n21. Phillips (1746), 205, notes that

the "tornado" is a sure sign that one is approaching the Guinea Coast and that he saw none south of the equator. These squalls occur commonly at the beginning and end of the rainy season. *Africa Pilot* (1967), 49. See also Bosman (1705), 112-14; Isert (1992), 210.

315 The harmattan is caused by the north-east trades-hot, dry air masses, coming down from the Sahara. They cause a sudden and dramatic change in climate, characterized by a decrease in temperature and humidity, resulting in a thick haze. The effect is often keenly felt in unusual dryness of the skin, irritation of the eyes, nasal and throat passages. Many sources describe barrels drying out so much that their staves shrink, leaving great cracks. Tilleman limits this phenomenon to February, but it often starts in late December, continues through January and into February. See Boateng (1970), 23-26, fig. 8, 9. See also Dapper (1670), 457; Barbot (1992), 456-57; Phillips (1746), 214-15; Bosman (1705), 114-15; Rask (1754), 198; Isert (1992), 210-11 for measurement of the drop in humidity during harmattan.

316 Tilleman has excluded February because of the harmattan (and he should have excluded January as well), and April-June because of the rainy season. Actually there are, normally, two rainy seasons at Accra, the principal one in April, May, and June, and the secondary one in September-October. See Boateng (1970), 32-35.

317 This probably signifies sea miles, 7.4 km. The distance would then be approximately 10,500 km.

318 Tilleman advises sailing south by east to avoid the currents in the Bight of Benin. De Marees (1987) 223 points out the extreme difficulty of getting out of the Bight at Fernando Po because of the strong east-by-north current, some ships having taken six to seven weeks to reach Cape Lopez, just south of the equator. See *Africa Pilot* (1967), figures B, C, D, E, which show the Guinea Current setting eastward along the coast as far as the Benin River, and a southerly current following the coast northward to the same place.

319 *Atlantic Ocean Pilot* (1884) map No.6 (facing p. 897) informs that "Approaching the African coast, Anno Bom [Annabon] Island is considered to be at all seasons in the Equatorial Current [setting west], Princes Island [Principe] in the Guinea Current [setting east], and St. Thomas [São Thomé], situated nearly midway between the two, as within the influence of one or the other current, according to the seasons." Bosman (1705) clearly preferred Annabon for trading and implied that ships went to São Thomé only by default, having failed to reach Annabon. See also Barbot (1992), 742 – 43; Jones (1985), 56-57.

320 Brun in Jones (1983), 74; Hemmersam (ibid.), 132-33; Phillips (1746), 248-49; Jones (1985), 197-98 good spices, etc. but bad water. For sugar from São Thomé, see note 331.

321 There are no large mammals on São Thomé. Alan Tye (personal communication). Tilleman may have seen the dead animals, or skins, or meat, acquired on the mainland and then brought to the islands for sale.

322 São Thomé was long an *entrepôt* for the Gulf of Guinea trade, the island's colonization and trade having been established in the 1480s. See Blake (1977), 93, 95 ff.; Fage (1969), 61-62. See also Lübelfing in Jones (1983), 14-15; Barbot (1992) , 736-37. The castle *São Sebastião* was built in the 1580s, and is subject to contradictory descriptions in the early sources. Groeben in Jones (1985) 56, writing in 1682, found it well equipped; Phillips (1746), 249, writing in 1694, found the walls "ruinous and weakly mann'd"; and Tilleman, in 1697 found it well equipped, There is no indication that Tilleman actually visited the castle, whereas both Groeben and Phillips did. Thus, it may indeed have deteriorated between those two visits and Tilleman's judgement may have been too generous. For Christians and Capuchins on São Thomé see Bosman (1705), 417-18; Jones (1985), 198. São Thomé had been awarded a bishopric as early as 1534. Vogt (1979), 52. The post of governor was evidently shared by "five viceroys, each of whom is the head for one year." Groeben in Jones (1985), 56.

323 Jones (1985). 57.

324 Bosman (1705), 418-19; Jones (1985), 211-12.

325 For a long description of the River Gabon area see Bosman (1705), 400-08. He also remarks that the water at a point (Sand Point) in the river is better than that at Cape Lopez. See also Roggeveen/Robijn (1971), 32; Barbot (1992), 721-25. For a multitude of parrots see idem 720 n3.

326 For wares exchanged in Sierra Leone see Tilleman [9].

327 Bosman (1705), 405-06, gives a completely opposite picture of the status of the prince, and king. He claims that no honor whatever is shown to either of them "and those Gentlemen have only the bare name of Royalty, without the least shadow of the thing itself." Here I am inclined to believe Tilleman's interpretation because of the added detail.

328 Bosman (1705), 402.

329 "On land" can by no means be interpreted as "inland." Tilleman's land journeys at that time would have taken place only in the coastal areas, where his business was conducted.

www.ingramcontent.com/pod-product-compliance
Lightning Source LLC
Chambersburg PA
CBHW071206070526
44584CB00019B/2933